One Eye Open

unir1

William S. Peters, Sr.

inner child press, ltd.

Credits

Author
William S. Peters, Sr.

Editor
hülya n. yılmaz, Ph.D.

Cover Graphics & Design
William S. Peters Sr.
inner child press, ltd.

General Information
One Eye Open
William S. Peters, Sr.

1st Edition: 2020

Publisher Information:
Inner Child Press International
www.innerchildpress.com

ISBN-13:978-1-952081-18-7 (inner child press, ltd.)

$ 19.95

Poets . . .
sowing seeds in the
Conscious Garden of Life,
that those who have yet to come
may enjoy the Flowers.

Dedication

To the minds that seek

And the eye that sees

And that eternal, energy infinite

That compels us

To continue to go forth

In the darkness of my life
I heard the music
I danced . . .
and the Light appeared
and I dance

Janet P. Caldwell

Table of Contents

The Poetry

Table of Contents . . . *continued*

Table of Contents . . . *continued*

Table of Contents . . . *continued*

Epilogue

Preface

Sometimes we do have too much to say . . . while at other times we say too little. And then there are the rare times of silence, from which I believe all things manifest. I seek out this silence only to find screaming voices waiting for me in the shadows, disturbing my much sought after peace. It is at these frozen moments between the footsteps of my journey that I find myself with limited choices . . . to write or to sleep. The sleep does not last long enough. I find what I chose to ignore does not go away compliantly. I can only calm the call of these wild vagrant waifs within me by picking up my pen.

This book is the result of such visions, seeking, and journeys into that vast realm of potential and the conflict that abides within the soul of this man. I can not say that my words offered throughout this manuscript will be readily meaningful to you, but they are to me. With that being spoken hopefully devoid of my ever-lasting companion, 'vanity', I give these words back to from whence they came ... the ether. May you enjoy the planting, the nurturing, the harvest and the fruit.

Bless Up

william s. peters, sr.
'just bill'

Notes from a Friend

Having had the privilege to be a friend to Bill for several years, I consider myself honored with his presence. I will remain eternally grateful to him for being an irreplaceable confidant, for our elaborate conversations on intellectual and spiritual levels, but also for our meaningful exchanges on world's various literary traditions and movements. Each one of those interactions has been a gift as far as the expansion of my overall worldview, and I shall always treasure Bill's contribution in that regard.

And then, there is his poetic art . . .

When I became Bill's personal editor years back, I knew immediately that his poetry could not and should not be confined to a conventional definition of the genre. In an introduction to one of his voluminous books, I refer to his style of creative writing as "Williamesque" (no relation to Shakespeare). In the wake of my multiplied intimate readings of his work, I insist on my conclusion. His diction, form, imagery, content and context most certainly stand out in a unique way among a multitude of poets I had been professionally analyzing over an extended period of time in painstaking detail.

Bill's poetic craftmanship demands a higher understanding and thorough appreciation of every nuance that he accentuates through his words, verse breaks, inner rhymes and line rhythms. What another editor might see as challenges in his compositions of verse, I embrace as a cherished present when this particular occupation of mine is concerned. Any editor in tune with the authentic voice of the author must, after all, avoid the unnatural restrictions that are placed upon a writer's creativity and poetic license by forcefully standardized rules of writing.

Bill's written art may be summarized as in the following: an effortlessly expressive and multidimensional authorial voice; a delicate understanding and refined use of the English language – with no apologies for obligatory colloquialisms or invasive diction, while bringing words into life and demonstrating how language prompts meaning for a text; a seemingly infinite command over universally relevant content of any nature, while providing a wealth of possibilities to serve content within the framework of symbolic and literal contexts; an instinctive delivery of context, and a mastery of the formalistic fundamentals of literature – with no interest in regurgitating the prescribed mechanics.

With 'one eye open' – the eye of oneness, Bill casts light on the darkness of the human construct as it arises from the depth of one's soul. Throughout this process, he does not shy away from self-revelations. The darkness, however, is short-lived in his poems. For he lays the greatest emphasis on love – love of and for all, love for the peace and healing of all. While he thus stresses the universal connection within humanity, he incorporates into his narrative a social critique of the entities of the past and the present as far as their problematic history. He then reassuringly projects on a harmonious change and a hope-filled future of oneness within all creation.

Bill's poetic eloquence and brilliance that I have attempted to convey to you, dear reader, find their accurate depiction in the following statement by Audre Lorde (1934-1992), Caribbean-American poet, essayist, novelist, and civil rights activist:

"Poetry is not only dream and vision; it is the skeleton architecture of our lives. It lays the foundations for a future of change, a bridge across our fears of what has never been before."

hülya n. yılmaz

Poets, Writers . . . know that we are the enchanting magicians that nourishes the seeds of dreams and thoughts . . . it is our words that entice the hearts and minds of others to believe there is something grand about the possibilities that life has to offer and our words tease it forth into action . . . for you are the Poet, the Writer to whom the Gift of Words has been entrusted . . .

~ wsp

One Eye Open

unir1

William S. Peters, Sr.

poetry is . . .

Poetry succeeds where instruction fails.

~ wsp

The Poetry

I FLY
because I Can
...said the Dreamer to the world.
www.iamjustbell.com

A Piece of Peace

But a small slice,
But a crumb
That I can savor
That lasts me
For but a while . . .

I am the earth,
I am the sky,
I am the forest, the wood,
The valley, the mountain,
The rivers, streams, brooks, and seas
I am the wind,
I am the breath of life . . .

I, we, see everything

I am all the creatures
Upon this planet,
That crawl leap, swim, float, slither, fly and climb
Beguiled by men
Sublimely so . . .

Disease and famine . . .
The makings of war,
With bombs and bullets
Shredding and shrouding
The atmosphere.

Can we not coexist?
Is not there enough
For everyone?

Whose sons,
Whose daughters
Will push the button next?
Whose sons,
Whose daughters
Will suffer the consequences
For which there is no defense?

I ask you not for much.
Do I?

Just a piece of peace . . .
And let us all heal together!

Freedom

Where does it exist?
In what deluded realm
Does such an enigma live?

What are we 'FREE' to do,
Save possibly think
Our own thoughts?
Even they are built upon
A foundation of 'SUSPECT'.

Who amongst us is 'FREE'
To not breathe,
Eat,
Sleep,
Love?

Are not we all tethered
To the nurturing of
Mother Earth
And all of her
Expressive glory?

Born Again

April 8, 1951
Was the beginning of the demise
Of the world
As I should have known it.

Sure, there were good times,
Mesmerizing times,
Happy times,
Beautiful times,
Loving times, . . .
The only problem was
That I awoke.
I was filled with wonder.
I was curious.
Insatiably so!

At many turns,
Around many corners
Of many paths,
I was led to
Ask more questions
About why,
When,
Where,
What,
Who,
And why again.

I had a tendency
To seek,
Day in, day out
Every week.
Every year,
On and on.

Yes, I found many more wonders,
Treasures,
Laden with joys
And many tears,
Doubts,
Fears
And exhilaration,
Elation, deflation
That filled the equation
I applied
To my life.

This is my 'temporary' summation,
And it has been
For quite some time . . .
Sublime.

I strove
To harmonize my being-ness
With 'ONE'-note melodies.
Be the rhyming poem
To honor this opportunity
We call "life".

Through the strife,
The rife,
I was quick
To grab a conscious knife
And cut away all the things
That tried to cut me,
In such a way
That would hurt,
Or render me back to the dirt . . . death
Before I wanted to go.

There are so many ways to die
Besides physically . . .
Consciously,
Emotionally,
Spiritually,
And let us not forget
Hopefully,
But I never had a problem
With that,
Because I loved to dream
And believe
That I could achieve
Whatever I conceived.
How about you?

I have crossed that bridge
Both ways
Many a time,
That now I have
My own path
To death
And resurrection.

Yes, I have been born again,
And again,
And again.

Retribution

Some say that her visit
Is long overdue
Perhaps . . .
But she will arrive
On time,
Lady Karma
And her mime-show.

No one really knows
The time or place,
But each one of us
Must face her
In the court
Of reflection,
As she sorts
Through our lives.

Either you will be enraptured
Or filled with an unquenchable lament,
But your life will flash before your eyes.
No surprise here!
As we are captured
In the moment
Of retribution . . .

Live wisely.

Alternatives

Break the chains,
Examine your thoughts,
Step away
And imagine yourself
Untethered,
Unfettered
By opinion,
Perspective,
Judgment,
Indifference
And willful dissonance.

'Woke yet?

Watch the people,
Watch their reactions,
Busy like a colony
Of ants
Doing the bidding
Of the 'one'.

Step out of line,
And you will be
Dealt with.
Just because . . .

A 'New Age',
Not so new,
Is upon us
And has been
For quite some time.

Awakening,
Awakening,

Only to miss the false solace
Of sleep.

Free?
FREE?
Freedom?
Did it ever exist,
Or is it just some
Plasma-like feeding
We so eagerly ingest
To remain untroubled
By the possibilities
Of differentiating truths?

The youth . . .
Do they have hope?
For what may I ask?
Their task at hand
Is beyond those things
I and people like me
Demanded
Oh, so many years ago.

Keep your toes on the line,
I heard a loud booming voice say.
Today
Is the beginning
Of a new nightmare
Beyond the '101', son!

Choice?
A conundrum at best.
For the test put before us
Is to see if we have yet
To conform
To the indoctrinating paradigm

Put before us
By those slimy aliens, demons and miscreants.

Stuck in mental mud . . .
A mutual mire . . .

Like it is said,
When swimming in a sea of shit,
Keep your mouth closed.

What are the alternatives?

William S. Peters, Sr.

Monsters in the Garden

There are monsters lurking
In our once pristine gardens
Of civility,
Tolerance and acceptance.

There is a hole
In the bottom of the bowl
Of compassion.
So, we find great self-favor
As we exercise our inhumane flavor
When lashing out at others
Who are different.
Well, aren't we all?

Who stands tall these days,
Save edifices and buildings
Of our erroneous deceit?

The repleteness
Of our incompleteness
Is astounding,
As we as a humanity
Are floundering
In our own soured regurgitations
Of the soured meals of persuasion
We have ingested
Occasion after occasion
That cannot be digested.

I must confess.
Yes, I must.
For I too have violated
The trust
Of which we have been

Endowed with,
As we shift from the 'enough'
To wanting more
Than our needs.

The seeds of malcontent
Have been spent
All over the place,
Regardless of our fears
Of the 'morrow,
Or the tear-filled sorrows
Of our ludicrous, lascivious
Self-induced lament.

These monsters,
The monsters
Who lurk in the shadows
In our holy gardens
Are none other
Than ourselves.

Monsters in the garden . . .

The Science of Fi

I remember the days of
The Global Warming crisis
And how the people,
Including my self,
Questioned our world leadership,
The fossil fuel industry,
And all others
Who were in denial.

It was one of our coldest days
Of that winter, 2022 . . .
45 degrees.

I have always said,
"If we do not do something,
Something will be done."

The people, the masses
Had become taciturn
With their voice for change.
No one any longer knew
What to believe.

I believe the 'powers to be'
Had done an incredible job
Pandering their divisive subterfuge,
Laced with unverifiable rhetoric.
'Fake News', some called it . . .

Fake or not, something
Evoked a change
That affected us all.

Was it the water,
The Kool-Aid,
The food
Or the air
They laced with chemicals
From unreachable heights
That we could not
Reach,
As they breached our consciousness
With variegated deceits
And other mindful poisons?

Was it our fatigue
That came from
Fighting the demons,
Who controlled the planet
By way of our need for
An acquiescent sleep?

As I said many years ago,
In my poem penned
In the early 2000's,
"The Antithesis",
"We get what we deserve, don't we?"

Useless protests, petitions,
Social media, video games,
YouTube,
Reality shows airing
From 1600s,
Our halls of justice,
Political forums,
And on the streets of the Police State
Was a reckoning
That I reckon
We could not quite get

A handle on
Nor escape.
So, we now suffer the consequences
Proffered by lobbyists,
Greed-laden elitists
And other 'Orwellian' aspects
That have snatched the prospects
Of a bright future
Right out of the cradle
Of our dreams.

This is the "Science of Fi"
With a ludicrous preposition
Stuck in the middle,
Betwixt the dying prefects of potential
And possibility.

Revolution's window
Has passed us by
With not even a sound warning shot,
Capable of startling us all
Into a verifiable
Certifiable action.
Though there were many bombs and bullets
Being deployed
And employed
To keep our valor
Hidden in the shadows,
While our courage
Put its head
Under the covers,
It too seeking
A good revitalizing nap,
The ultimate slap
In the face,
As this may have been constructed

By design.
But it was our 'me time'-selves
And other partisan selfish motivations
That gave wings
To our demise
Right in front of our
Tearless eyes.

We have cried so much for so long
That the trail and the songs of woe
Had lost their import
And meaning,
While we were weaning
Off the teat
Of contentment and folly.

No more Jolly Ranchers for you
From Wal-Mart!

Shit, let me start this poetic story over:
"Once upon a time,
In the land of 'The Science of Fi' . . .

"Fi": The solmization syllable used for the semitone between the fourth and fifth degrees of a scale

Carlos Saavedra Lamas

He was the first
Of his land
To be acknowledged
As one who vied for peace.

In a world
That does not connect,
He did
Through his efforts,
His works,
His ideas,
His heart,
For the 'all'
Of humanity.

A Lawyer . . . Ph.D.
He taught
Constitutional Law.

A Minister of Peace,
Calling for the ceasefire
And unjust wars
Between nations . . .

Oh, how we need him,
His spirit now!

He brought Argentina
To the League of Nations
And became El Presidente
For us all.

A Nobel Peace!

Whether . . .

She was a Linus-type character,
Walking around
Sucking on her proverbial thumb;
Rain clouds over her head;
Holding, clinging tightly
To her blanket
Of false certifiable securities . . .
Insecurities . . .
A senseless sense,
Not worth 2 cents!

I wanted to be her sunshine.
Yes, I did.
But she always
Listened, then dismissed.
For her companion,
Doom,
Had become
Her best friend.

It is not that she did not know
Of joy
Nor mirth,
Nor a once-in-a-while
Smile of happiness.
No! Even she too
Knew
That deep inside,
Hiding away in the shadows,
Resided a solution,
Her solution
To all that she longed for,
Wished for,
Pined for,

Dreamed of . . .
But the trials of her life
Somehow relegated
A false sense
Of denial
That she was worthy of experiencing
Her greater self.

Whether the weather
Was fair or cloudy,
Stormy or pleasant,
Balmy or chilly,
She clung to her
Proverbial blanket,
Believed in her cloudiness
And sucked incessantly
On her thumb,
Attempting to be content
With the life she allowed,
Whether she liked it or not,
Never realizing fully
That the power to change
Was hers to demand,
Command
At will!

Dismembered

I ripped off both of my arms,
And then, my legs.
How I was able to accomplish this
With no arms,
I have not a clue.
But somehow
I was able to
Disable my 'self'
In such a way
I could no longer navigate
As I was supposed to,
According to this world . . .

I then attempted to detach
This head of mine
That spawns
Far too many thoughts
That are not productive
Or serve my best interest.
Whew, that was a task!
However,
The remnants of thought
Still prevailed,
And thus, began to multiply.

What have I done,
I asked my 'self'.
Surely, one cannot live
In such a way!

I could no longer walk
As I used to,
Nor could I hand-le
The things

That assailed me
As they used to.
I was a new man . . . I think.

I somehow sat up
And began to contemplate
This new theoretical position
Of mine.
Sublime as it may be,
And though my head
Was semi-detached
From the rest of me,
I was able to see
Things differently.

Now I know,
This is a crazy poem.
But consider,
Consider
How we walk through our world,
How we hand-le our lives
And our circumstances.

We have tried to detach ourselves
From ourselves
Many times,
But we find that we are still yet attached
In so many ways
That are not readily seen.
You know what I mean.
Don't you?

Ships

What kind of 'ship' are you sailing on?
Class-Ship
Friend-Ship
Kin-Ship
Ruler-Ship
Dictator-Ship
Freedom-Ship
Bias-Ship
Love-Ship
Sinking-Ship
Floating-Ship
Bull-Ship
Censor-Ship
Hard-Ship

1

Your struggle
Is that of mine own.
Your woes,
Your anguish,
Your fears,
Your doubts,
And all the things
That challenge your whole-ness.

It may take some time
Before your ripple
Reaches me
On my proverbial 'safe' shores,
But it shall . . . eventually.

We are all but a pebble,
Cast into the stillness
Of the ocean of life.

It may take some time
Before your ripple
Reaches me,
. . . but it will.

There is no escaping
That truth
That we are 1,
Of 1 species,
Of 1 creation,
Living on 1 planet,
In this 1 time.

It may take some time
Before your ripple
Reaches me,
. . . but it will.

A March Christmas

I remember the anticipation
That swelled in my imagination
As a child,
As I looked forward
To the Christmas Day-snow.

My parents bought me a sled,
And I was so anxious
To test my skills . . .
Speeding down the snow
And ice-covered hills,
Only to walk back up
That same hill,
To have another go.

I had waxed my runners
With Mommy's good candles
So that I could go extra fast.

I had oiled the pivot rivets and screws
On my handle
With Crisco
So that I could make the turns
This way and that.

Now, this same snow
From my yesteryears
Has been relegated
To be a nuisance . . .
Roads salted and sanded,
Plows plundering,
Setting asunder
The cold white dreams
Of every child.

Not to mention
The mild-ness
Of our winters
Since,
Hence.

These memories
Of times long gone
Are my own little private
Christmas in March.
A present in the present . . .

Who Are You?

My child,
Are you one of integrity
That travels the road of life
Sure-footed and true?

Are you one of
An unimpeachable honor
That clings not to custom
Nor rote,
Nor the interpretations
By men
Of the meanings
Of Suras or Scriptures?

Are you guided
By the chaste and contrite
Ways of the heart?

Woe be unto you,
Oh man,
Oh woman,
Should you be as a leaf
In the winds of life
That knows not
Which way your soul
Travels!

It is better to be
A rock, tumbling along
The stony pathways,
Or a grain of sand,
Washed by the waves
Upon life's beaches
Than a tree, rooted

In the quicksand
Of feebleness
Or insincerities.

Even mountains are moved
In the annals of time.
They come,
And they go
With the ways and movements
Of the millennium
Through space.

I ask,
Who are you ?
Do you know
Where you stand?
What you stand for,
Or why ?

Are your ways founded
In the heart-light
On which all creation depends?
Or are you but a shadow,
Lurking with others
Of thy kind
Living in fear of
The coming Sun?

Tell me, my child,
Who are you?
Are you one of integrity
That travels the road of life
Sure-footed and true?
. . . tell me!

A Tear for the Living

I shed this tear
With a hope
That it may clear our eyes.

I have many more . . .
Many
Flowed down that river of time.
Past . . .

I lament still
For that which is,
Was
And may come our way.
So, this day,
I shed a tear.
For I may be done, all dried up
Tomorrow.

A tear for the living . . .

Folly Afoot

In a world
Where virus besieges virus,
Pathogens attack,
Seeking to eradicate
That which they created,
And the fight is waged
By those innocents
At the doorway
Of destruction
And demise,
Who once were determined
To live vicariously
Through their dream-state . . .

Novel, you say?
In the interest of science . . .
Or is there some other
Ominous agenda
That leads us to this folly,
Where death raises its baton,
Orchestrating fickle fears?

A perfect symphony
Of wailing and grief . . .

Sing to me
The song of lamentations
That my tongue may taste
Its own bitterness.
For in the times
When voice was required,
It remained silent,
While demons stole

What little light of hope
Men once possessed.

Yes,
The folly is afoot,
Ravaging the fruitless gardens
Where possibilities of promise
Once were bountiful.

And now . . .
We wait,
Speculating outcomes,
While watching rainbows
Become monochromatic
And dullen.

And . . . all the petty, pernicious, paltry, perceived
Differences have been rendered ludicrous at best.

Movement

In the river of sound,
Where the bass collides
With the tickled contrast
Of the ivories,
I hear the snare of cymbals
Celebrating
With a stated smooth applause
Of Jazz.

There is a movement
That reaches in
And grabs my ethnic soul.
I hear and feel
The caress of the wisdom
Of my ancestors,
Urging me forth to indulge
In the rhythms
Of the world
And all of creation.

I am the Universe,
As are you,
And we undulate blindly
To the flow of energy
That emerges from within us
That embraces us
In a consciousness,
A movement . . .

Confession

He cried for his poetry.
He cried:

Lorde, you know it's me,
Who comes to you
With his humility
Intact.

The fact is that
I have been humbled
As I went through life thus far,
And stumbled
And fell.
Yet you, my Lorde,
Did not forsake me.

Many lessons
Have I learned.
Many, I have not seen nor acknowledged.
Many more,
I refused,
As I recused my self
From your favor.

My Lorde,
This is my confession,
But it is not something
You do not already know.

You know my thoughts.
You know my heart.
You know my joys,

My desires,
My hope and dreams,
And my pain.

In this confession,
I am professing
My truth
Through my limited eyes.

I am still in denial
Of all the trials and tribulations,
Past,
Present
And those to come.
Yet
I do know that
Sometimes
You allow me to think
That I am alone.
But deep within,
I know that I am not,
And never have been
Without you.

Little Men

The encampments
And the mass burial pits
Have long ago been dug.

The plastic grave-liners
Have already been manufactured
And stored . . . waiting.

The patents have already been granted
For the cure.

Yet another vaccine
To serve the purpose
Of wealth creation . . .

Little men make viruses
To serve this end,
Negating the sanctity
Of life.

More bail-outs
For those who do not need them . . .
And again,
The little man suffers
For their cause.

Little men speaking in tongue,
Words they themselves
Understand not,
But they say them just the same.

Elect a little man
As our leader,
And we shall all go

The 'little way'
For the rest of our lives.

Little men of all types,
Creeds,
Cultures
And conundrums
Beating the drums,
While screaming in their hearts
For deliverance
From the heavy boots
Of oppression . . .
But who is it
That hears their
Songs of anguish?

Little men
Stealing the eggs
From the hen house,
Hoarding them all
For a profit
They will never live to spend,
But would gladly lend
That they may exact
Yet another form
Of 'Usury'.

Collusion and complicity
Do not make the fruit ripe,
And sour fruit
Makes not
A sweet pie.

Artificial sugars and sweeteners
Will suffice, they say.
Even if the day comes

When they all get sick,
We have yet
Another vaccine
For this temporary malady
Until they die.

Little penis-ed men,
Seeking more false virilities
For their wilting libidos,
Thinking little thoughts of
Viable futures
Outside of the market,
Pander and market
Their soiled soul-ful ideas
And ideologies
Of what they think
The world should be.

I guess, they didn't get the memo:
God did not retire,
Nor is HE dead.
So, there is no vacancy
That any reprehensible reptile
Can fill.

Little men dancing
In the board rooms,
As they water-board away
Our last vestiges
Of decency,
Seeking a confession
That does not exist,
That we too are complicit
To our own suffering . . .
But are we?
Are WE?

They want an obeisance paid of sorts
That they are superior
To us all,
That they are 'supreme beings',
But never from my lips
Shall such come.
For all I see is
Little demonic men
Who have sold their souls
And hope to pay their way
Out of the coming apocalypse.

Woe be unto you,
O, little man!

And then . . .
There are the 'boys with their toys'.

The Peace I Deserve

France and Germany
Working together,
Foreign Ministers
Aristide Briand, Gustav Stresemann
Being the iconic figures
For peace . . .

In the Swiss town of Locarno in 1925
Is where the agreement
Was signed
That gave each country
A bit of respite,
And each individual
Honor.

It seems to me
That 'Peace' should be
The natural way of man.
Or am I delusional
In my thinking?

At any rate,
We celebrate those
Who are the figureheads
That grant man the peace
He deserves.

Where are the peace merchants now?

Fontaine

There was Henri La Fontaine,
Who was not from Spain,
Who won the Nobel Peace Prize.

The year was 19 and 13.
Yet peace, we have not seen.
But he did manage to open a few eyes.

A Lawyer, a man,
A Barrister, they say,
Who argued the wisdom of peace.

Yet unto this day,
The world is in a fray,
And the wars have yet to cease.

He begged and he pleaded,
But few nations heeded
That war is as ludicrous as they.

Keep hope alive
And strive, o human, strive!
We will have peace someday.

So, it is not always the prize
That opens one's eyes.
You have to feel it in your heart.

Tolerance and compassion
Are a much-needed action,
And from our ways we will part.

So, I thank you, Mr. Fontaine
For addressing the inane.
For insanity must not rule our way.

And as I as well keep saying,
We must stop the little boys playing,
And soon, world peace will be TODAY.

Much Work to Be Done

It was a moonless night.
The demons of darkness
Still eerily crept,
Looking for shadows of consciousness
That they may whisper
Conjured deviance
Into the dreams of men.

The silence was a song
That brought anguish
To the uncertain wanderers
Who cast aside their faith.
For their empirical sight
And perspectives
Were their 'Holy Grail'.

The mailman was late
Yet again this day.
Where is my check
That liberates me
From my mental
Self-induced bondage?

I am hungry for something,
But I know not
What it is.

I thirst as well,
But all that I drink
Sates nothing.

I am alone and lonely
With no one
To speak with
About my abiding fears
That I will never understand
Who I am
And what purpose
I was sent here to serve.

So, I walk forward
Aloofly,
Trying my best
To pay attention
To the circles I wear
Into the soils
Of this 'holy' garden
We call "life".

What type of fruit
Shall come from my seed?
Shall it be pleasant
To the palate,
Or bring forth
A distasteful face
For its bittersweet
Misguidance?

I long to once again
Be caught up
In the euphoric rapture
I envision,
One that leaks from distant memories
Of a time long ago.

The nightmare has just about
Consumed me,
But I will not let my candle within
Be extinguished.
No, I WILL not!
For there is still
Much work
To be done,
Much work to be done,
Much work to be done!

Desire

Take not that which you dislike,
Nor that which you do not want
Into the
New Day,
New Year.

"Today is the first day of the rest of your life",
As is tomorrow,
The next day,
And the next.

Do not waste nor squander
Your opportunity,
Our opportunity
For change,
A change for the better.

It is your choice,
Your voice,
Your choice
To be that which you desire.
What do you desire?

Though we may never forget,
We can forgive.
Forgive others,
Forgive your self,
And let your joyful expectations
And intent
Be met

This NEW DAY,
This NEW YEAR
By your greater self.

What do you desire?

The Divide

I listened to some lyrics,
And I hear it . . .

I listened to the news,
And I hear it . . .

I listened to the rhetoric,
And I hear it . . .

'The Divide'

Genghis knew it.
Machiavelli knew it.
Shaka knew it.
Saadeddin knew it.
Augustus and Constantin knew it.
The West knows it . . .
Now.

Never affront the strength
Of a superior force
Unified!
"Divide and Conquer" . . .
That is the way to topple regimes.

We, the people
Have been turned
Against ourselves,
And we somewhat willingly

Ascribe,
Assimilate,
Accept
And acquiesce,
As it was planned.

We think that we have awakened.
Yet we still sleep,
But differently
Than we have ever before.

'The Divide'
Has our souls
Being cast
In the abyss of nothingness,
Where life-sustaining substances
Are void, defunct and absent.

There is a wedge betwixt us.
Or should I say,
There are many
That pit us
One against another,
Sister, brother, father, mother . . .
And others?

When will we truly awaken
And see 'The Divide'
That even pits us
Against ourselves?

'The Divide'

Anatomy of a Terrorist

No, I am NOT a terrorist,
But you still want to shoot me
In my face,
Shoot me anywhere,
Because of what I represent
To you.

Speaking of terrorists . . .
It is you.
Yes, YOU,
Who terrorize me
And people like me
And the world over!

How to spot a terrorist:

Are they wearing a uniform?
What color is it?
Blue . . .
Grey . . .
Black . . .

What is their eye color?

Rhetoric says,
Do they speak a different language
That you do not understand?

Do they look differently than you?
Yep, they may be a terrorist,
Or a drug dealer, a rapist . . .
At the very least.

Certain Terrorists MO (modus operandi):

Yes, certain terrorists
Have terrorized
Peoples,
Indigenous and otherwise,
All over the globe
For centuries,
And continue
To do so to this day.

They do this with labels
Such as,
In the name of
Humanity,
Liberty,
Human Rights,
Democracy
And . . .
Self-enrichment.

We do understand
Succinctly
Who the real terrorists are
With their
Forked tongues,
Unspoken agendas
To oppress,
Suppress
And exterminate
Any faction of humanity
That is counter,
Or gets in the way
Of their maligned purpose(s).

You, yes YOU
Terrorize
In so many ways . . .
With
Economics,
Disease,
Vaccines,
Laws,
Guns and bombs,
Housing,
Pharmaceuticals,
Food additives,
Rhetoric,
The News Media,
Religion,
Education,
Famine,
Water . . .

And the list goes on and on and on . . .
Ad infinitum

In-between

In-between the branches
Of the trees of the wood,
In-between the leaves
Dangling from its limbs,
In-between the silence
That permeates its self
In a contemplative majesty,
There is a breeze
That channels the gathering,
Whispering rote-ful incantations
Laden with music and poetry.

Can you feel it . . .
In-between?

In-between our thoughts and our breath,
In-between each heartbeat, each pulse,
In-between the fluttering and blinking
Of the eye of all of Man,
There is something divine
Begging to be recognized,
Clamoring for your attention
And embrace.

I am lonely, said the world,
Though you are here . . .
You are not.

In-between the footsteps,
The facial gestures,
The smiles, laughter and tears,
The anger and the indifference,
The advocation and aspiration,
The stumbles and falls,

William S. Peters, Sr.

Our experientialness goes
Unnoticed.
For we are busy with things.

In-between the petals
Of every flower,
In-between the 'cocka-doodle-doo'
Of every rooster,
The chirps of every bird,
There again is that void-less void
Shouting and crowding
My unconscious longings
For fulfillment.

In-between
My dreams of the day,
Those of my nights
And the frights of REM,
I see
The little imps smiling.

Yes, perchance we all
Should pay attention
To the handwriting
On the wall . . .
Can you hear the call
From the . . . in-between,
In-between you,
In-between me?

A Passing

Sitting here, reflecting,
Contemplating,
Examining,
Considering
My experiential-ness,
Being circumspectively careful
Not to get the foot
Of my consciousness ensnared
By that little impish me
Who lends himself to judgment . . .

Looking back,
Looking ahead,
Looking at
Where I stand,
It is hard to be conclusive
As to what the meaning
Of my life is,
Should be,
Or what end I strive or pine for.

Inclusive versus exclusive
A presumptive preclusive oxymoron . . .

I do know
That somewhere within the recesses
Of who I vainly perceive myself
To be
That I wish
To leave a few notes
Or clues
That I did come this way.

William S. Peters, Sr.

Sure, I have children,
Two handfuls of grands
And a great grandson as well.
But what would they tell
To their own
Of what they have known
Of my existence?

He was a good guy.
He was a poet, a writer.
A peacemaker, a fighter . . .
He believed, he condemned.
He condoned, he damned.

He loved, he hated.
He took chances, he waited . . .
Too long.

What was that song he always hummed?
Who knows? But he did hum along
With some music.
It appeared
That only he could hear it.

He was courageously
Filled with a fear
Of what he would become,
Of what we would become.

To sum it all up . . .
I am not quite so sure
If my cup
Was half empty,
Or half full,
Or if it makes a damn bit of difference.
But I do believe

I had,
And still have potential.

The essential thing I attest
About living
Is in the giving
Of one's self
To the effort of pretense.
Hence, why bother otherwise
If one cannot surmise,
And persuade themselves
To engage
In the exploration
Of possibilities and potentialities?

The surrealities and fiction
Have their own derelictions . . .
Darkness, light and
Truths
That transform themselves
From the age of consciousness.

Conception to the grave
From our youth
Until we save ourselves
From our selves . . .

And here I am,
Still attempting to drown out the dissent
Found in those whispering voices
That tell me
There are little choices
That I have
To be other than
What I am told
By that around me,

Which surrounds me
Within
And without.

Somehow,
I have mastered the ability
To doubt myself
And all that
I could have been
And still yet can be.

Funny thing about contemplation and reflection . . .
The process of certitudinal detection
Of what truly is,
Is as kaleidoscopic
As it ever could be.
For thoughts
Have no boundaries.
No, they cannot be contained
As we would like them to be.
For they are only passing
A passing-through
Once again.

Lights, Camera, Action!

We deludedly create fixations,
Telling our selves that our psychic libidos are
Unimaginably huge.

We build houses of esteem
Upon the quicksand
Of our hopes,
Internally praying
That we won't be found out.

We inhale the pride of others,
Stick our chests out
Like cocks in the chicken yard
During a feathered estrus,
Seeing our selves different,
Superior
To our contemporaries.

Like a Puff Adder,
A snake,
We look at life
And we puff at her,
Believing our feeble demonstrations
Of our imposed virilities
Persuade her
To do our bidding
For that false sense of superiority,
While all the while
We are shaking,
Quaking inside,
Hiding out from our own truths,
And not wishing to confront them.

But we cannot escape such things.
Can we?
So, we continue trekking down
That yellow brick road
That we have painted
With masculine overtones
And hues
So that we cannot in our waking
Accuse our little men inside
Of cowardice.

We do have intermittent self-talk
And debates of reason
Which we somehow
Always manage to win.
For we tell our selves
That, being made in the image of GOD,
We are the Lordes of our escapisms
And tomorrow, we will change
And gather our insecurities
And cast them into the pits
Of our Hell,
And set them afire.

We know, we are the liars,
For that day never seems to arrive.
So, we take our newly established
Weakened resolutions
On a test drive
To see how everyone else
Responds to
Our freshly penned plays.

Lights, Camera, Action!

Let us begin again,
All to add a few more inches
To our libidos,
Masturbating into the winds of futility.

What to Do?

My soul cries out
For a peace
That I can
Only faintly remember.

The excruciating anguish
Of its absence
Is becoming unbearable.
I, we, must do something!

The dire need for change
Is beating loudly, discordantly
Upon the drums . . .
It once concorded its self
With life's symphony,
But circumstances
Have now burned the score.

The Great Conductor
In the sky
Is sleeping,
Waiting for the flawed composition
To be re-noted.

Another Sabbath day, I guess . . .

The arrangement now
Being played
Assaults my ears,
And insults
My divine cortex.

Oh, what to do?
What to do,
I ask you.
What to do?

William S. Peters, Sr.

And I Come to You

Death does not always ride a pale horse.
Does he?

I have seen death myself
Come with fanfare and pageantry,
As I have also witnessed him
Sneak into the breathing room
And shut down the machine,
Grab the heart of the noblest
And the feeble,
And squeeze the last heartbeat
Into submission.

Who amongst us knows
His secret name
That we may utter it
And have mastery
Over his procession?

And I come to you . . .
Until the end.

Futile

I struggle with the demons
I have allowed within my self.

I struggle with the angels
Who struggle for my health.

I struggle to reach for the things
Upon the high shelf.

I struggle.
I struggle.
I struggle.

Futile . . .

Why? Because I have already won!

Small Circles

Co-centrically we exist.
Yet our lives mean naught
To those who think
They control the whole.

Willing to move a pawn
Or a million
Off of the game-board
Of life,
So that their agendas
May be accomplished . . .
But they acknowledge not
This truth:
Everything is connected.

They have yet to discover
This meaning
In its entirety entirely.

Life, death, birth
In reverse,
Or in any order you wish
To arrange it,
Are still the same thing:
Experience.

For any beginning
There must be an end.
And for every end,
There is something
That calls
For its own demise.

I opened my eyes,
And I began to see.
I closed my eyes,
And I began to dream
Of a different me.
And I was empowered
Like the blossoming flowers
That come this spring time.

I too have a fragrance.
I too have a pollen
That need to be spread.
I too have a nectar . . .
Some sweet,
Some you do not wish to
Touch thy tongue,
Or ingest.

In small circles,
Thoughts are revisited
Time and time again
Until momentum is gained,
And they influence
The whole.
For it is all connected.
Is it not?

Small circles

Curiosity Never Killed Any Cats
That I Know of

He cautiously dipped his foot
In the cold stream of consciousness,
Because he was curious
About how it felt.

The shock he experienced
In the sensory transition
From being warm and comfortable
To his senses being stimulated
Beyond his aforementioned comprehension
Was astounding
At the very least.

He began to swoon,
Howl at the moon,
Listen to the tune . . .
The 'Sirens of Awaken-ness'
Played,
As his toes wiggled and splayed
Open
To experience
This new sensation
That offered a new height
Of elation,
As it maligned the equation
Of life
He once held tightly to.

At first, it was frightening,
For sure.

For the water was cold.
And as he boldly stood stolidly

Upon the supposed safe sandy / stony shores,
He had to question,
Why?

Should he go further in,
He asked,
Or should he withdraw
And continue to bask
In the sun's seemingly soothing shine?

No! He so much wanted to be
Illuminated.
So, he evaluated
The risk
Of being frisky
And just jumping in
To that stream
Of liquid consciousness.

In the end, he did just that.
And his logic simply was:
Curiosity never killed any cats that I know of . . .

Wealth

Growing up,
My parents did not have
More money in the bank
Than needed
To pay the bills,
Or buy the groceries.

Nor did we have a house
With many unused rooms.

Our family car
Was big enough for us all,
Sharing laps
Once in a while.

There were no seatbelts,
Or power steering,
Power windows,
Power doors,
Or automatic locks.
Who needed them?
We managed to do
Just fine.

We never locked the doors
To our home.
If we did,
How would visitors
Knock and enter?
I never did have a key
To our house.

Toys, hah!

A bat and a ball, maybe,
For the boys . . .
And a doll for the girls.
Make-believe
And imagination
Were the things
That built our character
And kept us occupied.

I most likely
Had a fondness, immeasurable,
For stone-throwing
And climbing trees.
I was quite good at it.
And then there were foot races . . .
Make sure your sneaker laces
Are tight. No tripping!

Mom always had a garden,
And Gramps did as well.
His was a whole lot bigger
Than I liked. Whew!
A lot of work
Goes into tending
A garden . . .
Almost all year round,
And all day . . . so, it seemed.

Perhaps that is where I learned
To be diligent
And vigilant.
I thank you both
For that lesson.

We spent a lot of our time
During the summer

William S. Peters, Sr.

And through the early fall
Canning
Fruits and vegetables
For the coming winter,
For meals
And sweet desserts.

I stole a few Ball Mason
Quart jars of peaches
Out of the pantry
In my day,
Solely to satisfy
My sweet tongue.

I reach for the words
To express the wealth
Of these few experiences,
But I stumble
As I humbly think back
With a filling reverence.

Senselessly,
During the journey itself,
I did not know
How profound
That road, my road would affect me.
But these days,
As I reflect
Upon relationship
With my
Father, my mother,
Grandparents,
Brothers and sisters,
Aunts and uncles,
Cousins and friends,
I realize quite succinctly

That I have been a very blessed child
Always.

Sure, there were moments
When emotions and words
Were askew
And not so pleasant to endure,
But through it all,
There was respect,
And most importantly,
Love!

Love was a natural investment
Given to me,
And it continues to earn
Magnificent dividends
By way of my own family,
Children,
Grandchildren
Great grandchildren,
Nephews and nieces,
In-laws,
And of course,
My acquaintances
And friends,
And every heartbeat,
Breath,
Thought and impulse.
And let us not forget
Dreams and
Imagination . . .

I am a wealthy man,
And have always been!

William S. Peters, Sr.

A Spring Day

Sister and brother,
6 & 8,
Sitting by the window,
Looking out
At yet another
Beautiful spring day . . .

The weather was inviting.
The sun was shining.
Yet
They were forlorn.
For what is the use
Of going outside
To play,
If you cannot play
With your friends?

They tired of the activities
That Mommy had invented
In the attempts
To distract them.
And TV was boring.

They had mastered all the video games.
So, they relegated themselves
Once again
To playing with
Imaginary characters,
Just like they used to do
On rainy days.

It Is Time

It was all in my head . . .
The joy,
The pain,
The fear, doubt and worry.
Being unaware,
I was in no hurry
To resolve
My broken psyche.

Something I learned
In growing up
Was that these are
The accepted modalities
Of our lives.

Get an education!
Or should I say,
Get the indoctrination training,
Never noticing
The waning of our spiritual self
That was vibrantly alive
Upon our birth?

For what it is all worth,
I wonder if
It is all worth it.

We die a bit,
A little
Every day,
Hardly listening
To the incarnate whispers
And what they are saying,

But we do know
They are there . . .
Everywhere,
Shining brightly.
But we do not see them,
As they attempt
To illumine the pathway
Meant for you,
For me.

The blind man stumbles,
The mute soul mumbles,
The cripple tumbles
And our divinity crumbles
Like a week-old biscuit
That is only good
For feeding
The hungry and vagrant waifs
We embrace within.

The greatest sin
We repeat daily
Over and over again
Is denying
That star-seed
Within
That was meant for us
To nourish
So that we could flourish
In this 'garden of purpose'
Where we have been planted.

Now mind you,
This is all in my head,
And it is beginning to leak out
Into my expectations,

My dreams,
My visions
And my nightmares.

I am striving direly
To let go
Of all of my accumulated
Self-induced woes
And illusory lamentations.
For I have come to the realization
That the summary
Of this equation
I have forced myself into
Just does not work for me.

You see,
I am much more than
You see,
I see,
Or have ever been seen,
And I do mean
To experience
My harvest,
The fruition of my wonder,
My unrest.

And that voice within whispered,
"Surely you jest."
In full rebuke,
I now earnestly and wholly
Reject and refute
All definitions

William S. Peters, Sr.

I have been taught,
The ones I bled for,
Cried for,
Lied for,
Died many times for,
And the ones I bought.
For
It is time.
It is time!

What It Is . . .

We live in a world
That peddles dreams
Of a better tomorrow,
Thereby rendering us all
Ambiguously ineffective,
While we teeter-totter
On the possibilities
Of the 'right' chosen path.

Sure, we work towards that end.
In the end,
We are subject to the
Consumerism
That captures our souls
In a 'push button',
'Like'
'News Feed'
'Selfie'
'Buy Now'
'Microwave'
'What about me'-existence.

The consistence
Of how it is going down,
As we continue
To slide down
That slippery slope
Of being
'Dumbed Down'
Is quite the norm
And oddity

. . . a conundrum ?

That perhaps
Will never be set
Upon that straight and narrow 'chosen path'
That lends promise
For the days to come.

It is . . .
'What it is'.

Because

Because one has knowledge,
Does not make them wise.

Because one knows how to love,
Does not make them compassionate.

Because one can criticize,
Does not make them a master.

Because one has those who would listen,
Does not make them a teacher.

Because one knows of words,
Does not make them a writer.

Because one can rhyme,
Does not make them a poet.

Because one can make a noise,
Does not make them a musician.

Because one can smile,
Does not make them happy.

Because one nods their head in agreement,
Does not make them commit.

Because one says 'yes',
Does not tell of their heart.

Because one speaks with surety,
Does not affirm a truth.

William S. Peters, Sr.

Because one sleeps,
Does not mean they are rested.

Because one dances spryly,
Does not mean they feel no pain.

Because one embraces,
Does not mean they are embracing.

Because one's eyes are open,
Does not mean they see.

Because one is elected,
Does not mean they are wanted.

Because one stands in the midst of a crowd,
Does not make them a part of it.

Because one stands alone,
Does not make them lonely.

Because one can think,
Does not make them thoughtful.

Because one can solve the problems of others,
Does not mean they themselves are void of the same.

Because one speaks harshly,
Does not mean that their heart is not softened.

Because one speaks warm and tenderly,
Does not mean their heart is not cold.

Because one is learned in all the scriptures, verse and suras,
Does not meant they walk the path.

Because one understands the manner and workings
   of all things,
Does not mean they can create.

Because one has the gift of creativity,
Does not mean they possess understanding.

Because one appears to be virtuous,
Does not mean they are not soiled.

Because one is thirsty,
Does not mean they will go to the well.

Because one is hungry,
Does not mean they will eat of the offered meal.

Because one possesseth all things,
Does not mean they are not lacking.

Because one prays diligently,
Does not mean their heart is contrite.

Because one listens,
Does not mean that one hears.

Because . . .

Because Man is the cause of his ways,
Does not mean he comprehends how to control
   that which he causes.

Because . . .

Metaphor

I want to get high,
Higher than any sky,
Above the clouds
And look down
With lament
On what I have left behind.

I want to smoke some trees
While on my knees,
Praying,
Saying things
That will transmute
My left-behind reality
Into a snickering type of affair.

I want to dance
With the nebulas
And black holes
That flutter in my psyche,
Offering my soul sideways
To the lateral realities
That sparkle
In the dark night.

I want to hold the moons of Jupiter,
All of them,
In the palm of my left hand
And let fate
Run its course.
For, of course, the course
Of the 'right'
Has failed us.

Which way to Andromeda,
I asked the beetle.
The butterfly answered,
Spouting some nonsense
About a reverse metamorphosis.

I smiled,
And crawled through
That tunnel
Where darkness
Was yet unborn.

I want to become the rain
And melt into my tears,
And cleanse all that is
With what truly 'Is'.

My God,
Do I want too much?

I want to write new rules
For metaphors
And similes,
And create
Stories, Fables and Quaint Little Tales
That are real
In this realm
Of my existence.

I want to read the stories and accounts,
One thousand years hence,
Of how we conquered
That which looms
Over our heads,
Stealing our hope
And burdening our children,

All of them,
With the world
We left behind.

I want to win
Within
And without,
And banish fear and doubt
For all time.

I want our lives to rhyme
With all that is wonder-filled
And awesome.

Some day . . .

A 20-20 vision

Crossbreed

I am a blend
Of Dreams and Nebulas,
Quasars and Black Holes
With a bit of Stardust
Sprinkled here and there . . .
For seasoning.

I vie to once again
Return to the heavens
Where I once roamed aimlessly,
Exploring, wandering,
Seeking new wonders
Moment by moment.

"Why am I here?"
I have often asked,
"What is the task
I supposedly have come
To accomplish?"

I am a 'Crossbreed'
Of the Gods and Empathy,
And my compassion
Cannot be controlled
For long.

This traipse
Through this dense vibration
Is a distraction
At best.
For this empirical expression
Is laden with fault . . . lines
That are destined
To crack

And will fall apart
At the seams.

It is no rocket science
For one to see
That there is something wrong.
For it seems to me
That the songs we sing
Are discordant
At best.

Our inharmonious orchestrations
Are not symphonic, in the least,
But chronic-ally
Giving cause
To re-think
The road we have travelled
To get to this point.

Go to the 'Soul-cupboard',
My fellow,
And pull the holy oil
Off the shelves!

We must re-anoint ourselves
With a certain meaningfulness
Of what eternal damnation embodies.
For, truly,
This is the path
We have been upon
Way too long.

As they say . . .
I, you, we are
Spiritual beings
Having a physical experience.

So, let us move from the shadows
Of the dastardly things,
Open the doors of our souls
And cast the darkness back
Into the abyss of nothingness
From which it came.

Shine thy light,
My fellow 'Crossbreed'!
Shine thy light!

The Secret

The student sat at the feet of his teacher,
The Sage, and asked:
"Oh, Great Master,
What is the secret of enlightenment?"

The Master smiled softly,
As he grabbed and stroked his beard
In his right hand,
Pondering
About which words
Would be most meaningful
To the spirit
Of this young neophyte.

You see, the Master
Had a problem
With the word 'secret'.
For he, at some base level, knew
That everyone knew.
So, therefore
It could not be a secret.
Could it?

Nothing new here!

Perhaps obscured and ambiguous,
Hidden in the shadows of one's soul,
Lurked the answers
To all that all sought.

Perhaps the obstacle
Was the heart of the 'Seeker',
Or how they formulated the questions.

Perhaps it was one's stubbornness,
Obstinate-ness
And unwillingness
To let go
Of the mercurial and variable definitions
Of self
And that of the world.

Perhaps the poison
We all have ingested
To validate our positions
Is that of perception,
And her sisters of trickery
And delusion.

Did the illusion inhibit truth,
Or just put it in a safe place
So that fools
Would never wield its power?

Where do I fit in,
Queried the Master
To himself.

And for the uncountable time
Or more,
The light once again illumined
In the consciousness
Of this wizened Sage,
And this 'light' spoke
Simply:
"I AM."

With this re-realization,
The words were found
And made forth their journey

To the tongue of the Master,
And he spoke:

Repeat after me,
I AM.
I AM the way.
I AM the path.
I AM the gatekeeper
To my holy garden.
I AM the toll-taker
And he who pays as well.

I AM the rewarded,
And he who gives such
To those who chances
To travel the way.

I AM the blessed
And the Blessor.

I am the knower of all things,
And clarity is mine
To claim.

I am the Truth
And I am the Lie.
It is I, not my "I AM"
That vies
For my authentic self,
As I travel through
The adopted subterfuge and rhetoric
And that which I create.

I have hidden 'my self'
From 'my self',
And that is a truth

That is evolving
Into my growing now-ness.
This is no secret,
And neither is the power
Of my 'I AM'."

Now after this speaking, the Sage again
Stroked his beard, now with his left hand.
For the right hand was willful.
And now, this speaking
Has become
The fate of his disciple,
As it had become his own
Many moons ago.

The 'Secret' once again
Has shed her
Cloak and clothing
And undergarments,
Displaying her nakedness
To all who would but
Take a longing peek
And see themselves.

The secret . . .

Evolution

Our false sense of certainty
Has obliterated
Our false sense of security
As life is evolving
Into a thing unknown,
But expected.
For it has been spoken
In the prophesies of old.

Are we awakening?
. . .

That was a question I continually must ask,
Reaching back in time.
For that magic
We once possessed
During the years of our innocence,
Like any other longing,
Remains as such . . .
A distance away.

The smiles,
The sunshine,
The rain,
The pain when our realities
Met not our expectations . . .

We learned to dream
Of being fulfilled.
As the soft and silent tears of disappointment
Spill
Within my core,

I sing to this soliloquist moment
That lasts forever
And an eternity.

I try my best
To avoid lament-fully looking back
At what I left behind,
And though I search,
I cannot find . . . yet
That key I seek
That liberates me
From this prison
Where I have dwelled
For oh, so long.

The music,
The song,
The dance,
The show
Still goes on.
But now I begin to question
Yet again
The validity
Of it all.

What part of the illusion
Is contributed,
By me, the author
To my experience?

What part do I claim
To be delusion,
Thus manifested
So that I can survive
This surreality of fealty?
Literature oft' speaks

William S. Peters, Sr.

Of such things,
Such as castes,
Feudal Lordes and Serfs,
Land Barons and Tenants,
Sovereignty and Servants,
Masters and Slaves.
But to whom is the tithe paid
By thy soul?

Again, I ask:
Are we awakening?

This may vaguely seem like evolution
To some,
But I swear
I have been here before.
I swear.

Looking for Magic

I looked over the edge
Into the empty well,
And wished for signs
To the contrary.

Perhaps a pixie, a fairy,
Some hairy magician,
Or aged sage
Would appear
And abate
This lingering fear
That is slowly
Consuming me
In my conscious moments.

An eerie feeling
That had me reeling
To and fro
Betwixt the clouds
And the storm
Began to take form,
And I closed my eyes.
For this was a truth
I created
But did not wish
To face,
Nor taste
The meal
It was preparing
For me to ingest.

I looked heavenward
And spoke
With a semi reverent arrogance

To the Gods.
I said:
"Surely you jest.
Is this another test?
If so,
Of what?
My faith,
Or my belief?"

I have no need of either.
For I am looking for . . .
Magic.

Do you have any to spare?

Disguised

Living the lies,
Deceiving self,
Wearing masks, . . .
Accomplished thespians . . .

Let us make pretend
That we are something
We are not.
Or let us make pretend
We are not
What we are.

Either way,
Let us pretend
And allow the pretense
To be the navigator,
The sextant
That guides our wayward ways
Through our lives.

Living the lies,
Deceiving self,
Wearing masks, . . .
Accomplished thespians
Gathered in life's theatres,
Vying for their turn
To perform.

And the Day Shall Come

We think we know not
What is to come,
Or if we will be here
To witness
The final breath of humanity.

But we still dream
Of the days of promise
When the children will smile,
The sun shines
After the rain and storms
Have come and gone.

We hear the chirping birds,
Watch the flowers bud and blossom,
As a celestial spring
Comes upon us
Once more.

The caterpillar
Has gone to sleep.
Winter passed,
Soon to awaken
As a butterfly.

They shall spread their wings
And take flight,
Giving hope
To those who can see
Through the illusion.

My heart pines for peace,
One that it remembers
From the eons past.

I have walked with anticipation
Through this life's garden
With you
And you
By my side,
Suffering through
The same uncertainties of truth
And knowing.

Rumi, Hafiz, Khayyam,
Christ, Buddha, Jubran,
Krishna, Tabrizi, Solomon,
Sa'di, Rabia, Lao Tse,
Ebna la-Hakim, Mother Teresa, Musa
And many others
Spoke of the heart's beloved
And the longing for a certain union
To be consummated
In the matrimonial bed chambers
Of their souls.

I too know of this hurt of being unfulfilled.

Break me
Completely,
And let me piece back my self
With a penchant for the whole-ness
From which I was made.

I now know how I, we
Have erred
In the concessions and allowances
Of our skirts
To be soiled
By want of empirical things.
I now stand here

William S. Peters, Sr.

In the field beyond horizons,
Beyond contemplation
And consideration,
Feet rooted in the casting-out
Of non-truths,
Growing roots
That shall take hold
In the bosom of Mother,
And we shall bear a
New fruit
That has yet to be seen
Or tasted.

And all who partake
Shall know of 'The Light',
And voice the words
That were once unspeakable
And require no reason.

Yes, I stand here,
And I declare
That the breads of heaven
Shall rain down,
Feed the hungry
And sate the thirst
Of all, we the children.

Yes, I declare,
And the day shall come.

The Next Time

I have stood upon
Many a bridge
Waiting to be built,
Waiting for me
To take the first step.

I have climbed
Many a nonexistent mountain
That existed only
In the realm of my deluded
Fears and doubts.

I have swum across
Turbulent oceans
Of despair,
Where I thought drowning
Was my best option.

I once painted the Sun black
Because its brilliance
Was soulfully disturbing.

I have locked my self
In many a room,
And swallowed the key
To my salvation.

I spat in a desert,
Then tried to suck
The sand's moistness
Because I realized
That I was thirsty.

I have pulled the wings
Off of butterflies,
While they were still
In the cocoon,
Waiting to become.

I have sat here
On what seems to be
This same old rock,
Contemplating
The same old things,
While reflectively examining
My lack of movement
And growth.

I smiled at things
I never considered funny,
But I smiled just the same
In the name
Of etiquette
Because all the other sheeple
Did so as well.

I painted my dreams in
Bright vibrant colors
To awaken to a life
Of an untouched decaying canvas.

I penned beautiful lyrics
Of poetic love,
Created angelic melodies
At will,
And I shared them with no one.

I have slept longer
Than I needed to

Many times,
And when I opened my eyes
To face my weakness,
I rolled over,
And pulled the covers
Back over my head.

Do not ask me
Why I did these things!
Perhaps bad choices
Have lessons
That can teach us
Of our deliberate
Ineptitude
And lack of
Fortitude.

But . . . I don't know,
Perhaps
I will take
Another nap.
Perhaps
I will feel better
When I awaken
The next time.

Betwixt the Numbers

Death is
No place for heroes,
Nor for the lauded or loved
Men or women.

It cares not whatsoever
About accomplishments,
Possessions,
Dreams of the past,
The present,
Or those yet to be . . .
Nor does it conjure
Consideration or concern
For the loved ones
Left behind.

Death has no empathy
Towards the
Pain and tears
And confusion it causes.
It does not rejoice,
Nor does it lament.

Though at times,
Death exhibits compassion
To those who suffer
In ways told
And untold,
Who is to know
The ambling, rambling means
Of 'Death'
When she or he
Is merciful, or not?

Surely, not we,
Who are left behind
To mourn absences
And empty places,
Missing faces
At our tables of life.

I say, LIVE,
While you are.
Live all that you can,
While you can.
For life
Is where heroes
Come to be.
LIVE, I say, LIVE!
For
Death is
No place for heroes,
Nor for the lauded or loved
Men or women.

Who amongst us knows of its purpose
For the aged,
Or the young?

Life is but a dash
Betwixt the numbers . . .
LIVE, I say, LIVE!

Betwixt the numbers
Is what we are remembered for.

Live!

The 'Gateway' is open,
But the blind
Are the only ones
Who can see.
For if your eyes behold
This world,
You can view nor envision
The 'Light-Illumined Portal'
(L.I.P.)
That leads us to
The 'Rainbow Bridge'.

How many years,
Millenniums,
Eons
Have the saints, mystics and foretellers
Prophesied errantly
About that which is to come,
When it has been here
All along?

Tell me, o, child of creation,
Are not you
The Creator
Of the path you walk,
The dreams you conjure
And the longings of your heart?

Tell me, o, child of the universe,
Can you not lose
Your consciousness
And walk upon the

One Eye Open

Galaxies,
Nebulas,
The Star Systems,
The Moons
And illusions
You behold?

Behold the wondrous magnanimity
Of who you truly are!
Live not thy expression,
Cloaked in a self-woven cloth
Of ill-deceits
Of your own making
And that of others
Who wish you to but follow them
Into their chosen paths
Of perdition!

You alone
Are the condition
Of your resurrection,
Your erection,
Your coronation
That place you on the
'Throne'
That gives you sovereignty
Over your life.

Life is about
Your selections.
Choose wisely,
And be authentically true!

Live my child, live,
As you were meant to be.
Live!

This is the year 2020,
Time for you to see clearly.

Ebbing

Unknown fears,
Dauntingly haunting
The awakened
And the sleeping . . .

Shadows of doubt creeping,
Leaking,
Seeping
Into our sunshine,
Yours and mine . . .
Mixing some quinine
With the hard liquor
To help make it
A bit more palatable,
But the outcome is
The same.

In the name of Jesus, Buddha and Mohammed,
We live,
We die,
As we vie
To embrace the lies
We are.

We bed
Our desires,
And their lust-filled fires
Consume us,
As we rote-fully
Speak the words,
"In God We Trust".

The waxing and waning
Of what once was sane

And is no more . . .
Or was it ever?
Was the craziness
Just incubating,
Waiting
For an opportune time
To strike?

The webbing
That ensnares us,
Our hearts,
Our souls,
Our consciousness
Marches forward
With a calculable deliberate-ness
To create and maintain
A mess about us,
As we nest
In our false sense of illusory
Contentment
And delusory sentiments.
Ebbing at best, I say . . .

The Flickering Light

She sat by the candle
In the darkened room,
Mesmerized,
Enchanted
By the flickering
Of its light.

She oft wondered
About the shadows
That danced about.

She was but 8 years of age,
But she was filled
With an insatiable wonder,
A quest,
And she had questions
Yet unanswered,
Many
Yet to be formulated
Deep within
The recesses
Of her virgin-like thoughts.

She was compelled
Under the spell,
Lacking the forethought
Of absolution.
She needed to
Seek out a binding resolution
That would abate,
Quell
This deep stirring
She woke to each day,
Went to bed with each night

William S. Peters, Sr.

And dreamt about . . .
Day and night,
Night and day.

Her slumber was fitful,
Even when she was awake.
For she could not settle
For,
Nor blindly accept
The rituals
Or redundancies,
Nor rote
That was shoved in hers
And other's faces
On a daily basis.

She knew there was more,
She just knew there was.
For she heard the voices,
The whispers
That softly spoke
As an innate intuition.
Yes, she did.
And she, if not anyone else,
Was a believer.

She believed she could fly.

Do!

If you dream,
You begin to hope
That these dreams
Will become true.

If you hope,
You begin to believe.
For there is no other path
Except to . . .
NOT!

If you believe,
The only thing left
Is to open the door
Of your prison
And step outside,
And . . .
DO!

Reaching

Empty hands
Caress my soul,
Reaching to be filled.

I have turned, tilled the soils
Of my garden
Many times,
Searching for
That something
That can fill the void within
Somewhere between my
Love and self-righteousness.

Perhaps I am deluded
To believe
That there is more,
When I should learn
To simply be content
With what is already 'is'.

Like Isis,
I too raze as we rale
Against the inevitable-ness
Of reality
In my attempts to shape it,
As my self-created vision
Dictates.

I join with you.
We join together
And we come to a truth
That we are truly

Autonomous individuals,
Seeking congruity
With an elusive certifiable actuality.

Actually,
We are all lost
In our own perspectives.
Sometimes willing to be malleable,
Most times not.

Will we ever experience
A true unification
Of the spiritual aspects
That allows us a
Clarity,
Humanity,
Compassion
That are not marginalized
By the rhetoric
That abides
And that which is created?

The subterfuge is a great swell
In the ocean of consciousness
That drowns all
Who dare take a swim.

The undercurrents are a mighty foe
That sweeps us
To distant lands of hope
That seem to melt away
When we reach . . .
When we reach,

And we continue still
To sing that God-spell song,
"We Will Overcome".

Believe in the reaching . . . it is all we have!

Wondering

Where is our imagination spawned?
From what dimension
Does it come to be?

What are the properties of the equation
That ripen the fruits
Of our thoughts, visions
Or dreams?

What is the 'Mad Science'
That reveals the formula
Of manifestation?

I am just wondering.
Yes, wondering,
As I meander, wander
Through the fields,
The plains,
Across the valleys and mountains
And the vast oceans of
The possibilities
And potentialities
Of what we could be
Versus what we are.

Do you wonder like this too?

Be It Known!

You have never been a burden.
You are not heavy.
You are my brother, Brother!

We have struggled.
We have endured.
We have marched.
We have fought.
Some have been bought.
We have cried.
We have died.
We have lamented,
As our anguish continues
To ferment.

But know
That the fine wine
Comes in time
And will inebriate the senses
Of the non-senseless
And some senseless,
Who believed
We meant less
Or were less
Than human.

You, man,
Are my brother!
Whether you know it
Or not,
Or forgot
That we are all

On the same boat
That floats upon the oceans
Of life.

So, I must ask:
Why all the unnecessary strife
And undue rife?

But don't worry!
We have survived
Since the beginning
Through
Losing and winning.
The Saints a sinning,
As many still do,
And through it all
We will answer the call.
For it may appear
That you are heavy,
But just the same,
You are my Brother!

This excludes all
Demons and devils

Be it known!

Sanity

What the fuck have they done,
Making viral diseases
That somehow ease
Out of containment
By supposedly sane men
Who never want you to blame them?

A different type of sanity
Assails our human vanity
On this planet we
Inhabit.

Our habits will be our downfall.
For we hear not the dire call
That we all
Are stuck on this 3rd rock
Together.

They attempt to play God
And manipulate the weather.
Earthquakes,
As the 'News' fakes
And the world turns . . .
Someone is going to burn
In Hell for this
Because Karma,
The Universe and God all
Insist
Upon reconciliation
And balance.

Perhaps sanity
Will be restored.

Consciousness

It is our ruler,

Our jailer,

Our liberator,

Our emancipator . . .

Apply it well,

Or not at all!

Travelers

We passed each other
Along life's pathway.
We were going in different directions
Towards the same destination.

We were not twins,
But we were identical
With not a comparative flaw
Between us.

He was my 'Dream Catcher',
And I was his Muse.
Together but separately,
We created untold dimensions,
Laden with possibilities.

We searched to and fro
In whatever way we went.
We go,
Looking for what seemed to be
That elusive coin
That paid the toll
That we may cross that
Magical bridge
To the never-ever land.
Or is it ever-never land?
I always get stuck
On that mental conundrum.

Well, back on the farm,
Where the cows grow feathers
And the chickens moooo,
I thought, I saw another reflection
Of me, of you.

But it did not matter.
For neither the goats,
Nor the horses
Laid any eggs for breakfast.
But the pigs did prepare
Some vegetarian sausages
And bacon. Awesome . . . I think.

Traveling in the endless valley
Of 'mind-stuff',
Stuffing my potential
With exponential-ness . . .
Oh, what a mess!

We have the ability to create
Within ourselves
And without.

No room here for doubts
Nor fears,
Nor the counting of the years
Gone by
Or those to come.
For time is as malleable
As I wish it to be,
As is the direction I journey.

There is Me, Myself and I,
Walking the pathway of life,
Oft times
In different directions,
Though towards the same destination.
Whatever that is . . .

William S. Peters, Sr.

For the Peace of It All

Funny, how we all vie
For the same things.
Perhaps . . . not.

There is a healing needed
That our humanity may shine forth
As it was meant to be.

A world of peace
Is achievable.
Is it not?

If we can dream
Of a life
Where strife is a stranger,
Why can we not
Accomplish this end?

To feel safe
And not threatened
By the tenants of greed
And other covetous avarices,
Afforded to us
By those who always demonically
Want more . . .

Sustainability

I had a conversation with a passer-by who taught sustainability at the college level. After our intense and insightful interchange, I began to think about that simple yet oft' incomprehensible word 'sustainability'. I asked myself, *just what are we looking to sustain? Or, should the word be "to preserve"?* We, from generation to generation, are quite reluctant to hand over the reins of control of ideological tampering and implementation to the younger up-and-coming class of human beings, though they offer in many situations fresh looks and ideas that contribute to the betterment of the 'all'. We, the older generations, have become firmly entrenched in the superfluous status quos that we inherited from those before us. So, again I ask, just what are we looking to sustain?

Is it the suffering,
The pollution,
The smog,
Our blog,
The demise of the species,
Or the rise of the lies?

What lies before us?
Can we trust in it?
Shit! Quit!
It doesn't fit
Into my thinking.

Oceans of plastics,
Drastic wars and disease . . .
We can find no ease-ful way
Of living these days. Can we?

'Oh, say, can you see?'

William S. Peters, Sr.

What, I ask.
The task at hand
Is far graver
Than what we are told.

Souls being sold
For creature comforts,
But there is no rest
For the weary,
Just tear-laden hearts,
Set apart
From love.

So, again, I ask:
"Just what are we looking to sustain?"

The politics of it all?
The certainty of the fall
Of mankind?
What kind of thing is this
To seek to preserve?

If we are looking to save the planet,
Have no worries!
It will figure out a way
To save itself . . .
Sans humanity.
But we are not that humane,
Are we?

Evolving

He laughed at things
That were not funny.
He was filled with mirth.

He danced to a music
That no one else heard,
Unless they caught a glimpse
Of his soul.

He loved all things,
Even that which did not exist,
Simply because he could.

He sang.
He dreamed.
He played his way
Down the path
Of his life,
Sowing seeds
In a proverbial garden
Whose fruit
Was everlasting,
And always,
All ways,
Bitter-sweet.

He believed
That there was so much more.
No, he knew there was!
For that is life's promise . . .
Always evolving.

The Forecast

As minds across the globe
Are being lost,
Tossed into the
Mercurial,
Tumultuous,
'Winds of Change',
The children suffer
That of which
Is to come.

Hopefully,
That which is present
Will not last
Beyond these times,
The 'now'-times
Of our consuming anguish.

Death dances about us
In the streets.
The churches and synagogues,
The mosques and temples
Are singing unholy praises
Of a false cleansing
That panders to the
Demonic, deluded, demented souls
Who walk amongst us,
Pretending
That they are normal,
And that their agendas
Are spirited upon them
By some conjured image imagined
They call 'God'.

"Shalom",
Said the Rabbi
To the Imam,
And the Priest
Made a sign,
Signifying
A crucifixion
Which is due to shortly come.

Wait for it!

They say,
We know not the time.
Of what, I ask.
For the task at hand
Is already upon us.

I can no longer trust
With any particular ease
To be appeased alone
By waiting and praying.
IJS (I'm just saying).

Because
The cause
Is at hand.
If we pause too long,
The song, the show,
The performance
Will come to an end,
As will all the Thespians
Who pretend that
It, this, all was / is real.

Forecast:
Wait not for the answers
You already know!

You are the solution!

Chance

I give away a lot of books.
For, as a writer and poet,
My primary aspiration
Beyond writing more,
Is to be read,
And secondly,
Understood.
Perhaps . . .

Perhaps something I say
Will stimulate something
In someone else.

This desire of mine
Supersedes my desire for
Book sales,
Though that would be heavenly.
But heaven is an odd conundrum
That none of us may explain
Or describe.
We can only imagine . . .
Can we not?

So, I focus on what I can control . . .
Writing.
The rest is left to chance.
So, I give away
A lot of books.

Just Like Every Other Day

In my attempts to organize my thoughts
For this New Year,
There is this nagging feeling
Reeling in my head
About what I have
Left behind.

Look forward, they say,
To the new day,
The coming day.
But it is 'this' day alone
I must face,
Where change must
Take place.

Yes, I have chased dreams,
And it seems
That the faster I run,
They do as well.

Who amongst us can tell
When those 'Dreams'
Stop for a rest
That we can draw abreast
And indulge their presence
Like the 'present' to our lives
That we see them for?

So, as I said . . .
In my attempts to organize my thoughts
For this New Year,
I had no other choice
But to voice these concerns
That forever burn

In my spirit,
On paper,
In a poem
So that not only I
Can hear it,
But my ambiguous higher self
Can get the message . . .
As again,
The shadows
Come to life
And are dispelled,
Quelled
By my fortitude
Just like every other day.

I shall not fret . . . yet.
Maybe, if I can discover more of me,
I shall not fret . . . at all!

Discovery

She brought out my magnificence,
As I attempted
To bring hers about
As well.

We felt compelled
To share this gift
Of each other
With the world.

We journeyed.
We met many souls
Who beheld us
Where we are beholding . . .
In our hearts.

Yes, we love each other
And our sisters and brothers
As well.

From land to land
And back to our homestand,
We saw the sights,
The lights
By day
And by night.

We were embraced
By cultures discovered,
Uncovered
By the lovers
Of life.

Yes, there was strife,
But that did not stop
The children
From smiling,
And adults as well.

I cannot begin to tell you
About all
That we discovered,
Uncovered.

We were witnesses
To the greater aspects
Of what humanity is,
Can be,
And is becoming.

And all of this
Is . . . simply
Because
We danced
In our hearts,
As we were enhanced,
As we strove
To discover our
Magnificence
And yours as well.

Discovery

30 Pieces of Silver

Every Christian should
Thank Judas
For fulfilling the prophecy
That led to the resurrection
Of your salvation.

With God,
All things possess
A divine purpose,
And Iscariot
Could not
Exist outside
Of God's will.

These days,
History repeats its self
As the prophecy
Has been foretold.
Though inflation
Has made its mark
And the payoff
Is much more
Than
30 pieces of Silver,
The outcome
Is just the same.

With God,
All things possess
A divine purpose.
And Iscariot
Could not
Exist outside
Of God's will!

Haunting Memories

There are so many memories
Of past times . . .
Cherish-able
And
Those I wish not to face.

I can still taste the bitter
And the sweet,
As I reflect
On all the things
I did not complete.

There are words I did not say
That I should have said,
But I was too obstinate
And self-absorbed
In my own life
And my pity
To offer my pithy self
In obeisance
To that which my soul
Called for.

I left many chores undone,
Many doors sealed,
Closed . . .
Again,
Out of my own stubbornness
And unwillingness
To submit.

There are many tasks
I took on.
And I simply quit.

William S. Peters, Sr.

Perhaps I should have hugged myself more
And others as well.
There are many secrets
I still hold to,
That I will never tell . . .
Until that day of
Self-judgment.

Sentiments . . . I have hidden
From those I loved
And still do,
As I cry by myself,
In silence.

They haunt me at times . . .
These memories.

Sometimes they bring smiles.
Many times, tears,
Along with a longing
To return,
Go back,
And straighten that
Crooked path I tread.

I did dance a lot.
Perhaps at times
A bit too much,
But such things
Are what they are . . .
Faded tunes
That impugn me
To impugn my self
And all that I now see as . . .
My self.

These remembrances
Haunt me still
To this day.
And all that I am left to do
In seeking any semblance
Of resolution
Is to sing along,
As I attempt to harmonize
With the eerily
Haunting memories
Of days gone by.

To Me

I thought of you,
And I said,
At the very least
I could write a poem,
Declaring the depths of meaning,
Significance
And love
You bring
To my life.

The journey is unlike
Any one I have
Ever experienced before.

The light shines differently
In my heart,
And my thoughts
Are so much more
Loftier
Than
I have ever experienced.

I know I should thank you,
But how does a mere mortal
Such as I
Speak to an Angel
Who has brought such favor
To my ways?
Tell me, please!
How?

I dance differently.
I smile differently and deeper,
And my very soul
Has expanded beyond
My heretofore
Comprehension.

Euphoria may be an understatement.
Gratitude is but a word.
But you
Are here by my side,
Adorning my heart
Even in our parting
And lack of
Communal presence.

I know I should thank you,
But how does a mere mortal
Such as I
Speak to an Angel
Who has brought such favor
To my ways?
Tell me, please!
How?

So, I sing
And make this feeble attempt
At writing a poem
To tell you
What you mean
To me.

William S. Peters, Sr.

Front Lines

Guns, bullets, bombs and such . . .
Protecting a freedom
We never had.

The slaughter,
The killing
Of our brothers and our sisters
For false ideologies fed
To the unaware . . .

Shall we call it "patriotism"
Or something else?

I too served the agenda.
And then, I woke up
To see that my cup
And many like me
Were still empty
Of the promises proffered
By the rhetoric from
"The Land of the Free".

Protecting us from an invasion
That never came,
But from
Within . . .
The 1st being
The "Greed Merchants"
Who manipulate, exploit
The media,
Our government
And all else they can
To not just get all that they want,

But all that they see
In this 'Land of the Free'.

You see,
They and many who
Drank the Kool-Aid
Sincerely believe
That there is much to achieve
In the killing of others,
Our sisters, our brothers,
As we beckon to the agenda
Of those demonic others
Who use humanity
To fulfill their own demented inanity.
Insanity by any other name
Is still insanity.

Now, here we are,
Drawn together as 1
To face an enemy
That is capable of destroying
Not only all that we believe in,
But everything.

Think about that!

Yet, I bet
A dollar for a doughnut that
They, the merchants of all dastardly things
Are positioning themselves
Once again
To profit through the suffering
Of you, I, we.
Just wait and see.

William S. Peters, Sr.

We, again,
Are on the 'Front Lines',
And there is not a damn thing
We can do about it!
But do allow me to take the time
To salute
The true warriors
Who are working in our hospitals
And other 'essential' services
To care for perhaps
The last vestiges
Of our humanity,
As we 'Socially Distance' ourselves
From what we comfortably thought
We were.

Front lines . . .

Yearning

I have this hole
In my heart
That is sucking,
Draining away
The final vestiges
Of my hopes and dreams
Of a better life
For us all.

There are many challenges
Before us.
And our welfare
As a humanity,
Perpetrated upon us
By the Greed Merchants
And Demons
Who are never satisfied
With 'enough',
Is at risk.

There is a viral death
That approaches this epoch,
And it is biological,
But not how we believe . . .

It walks,
It talks
With its cunning
Forked tongue.

It sings songs
That soothe the anxious beast
Of malcontent

Which lives within
Us all.

It can even dance,
Laugh,
Lie,
Steal
Away the dreams
Of those not yet borne.

It is still yearning for more,
Even though
It already has
Most of what there is.

I am yearning for retribution,
Karma,
Balance,
And the death
Of this death virus
That has infected
The hearts of men
And women and children too.

Swing pendulum, swing!

I Consider This and These Things

On the edge of the precipice,
Looking into the abyss
Where rainbows are borne
And rainbows end,
I consider my fate
And the path
I have travelled.

What have I left behind?
Will my footprints fade into oblivion,
As time proceeds
Towards its never-ending destiny?

Will I be remembered?
If so,
By whom
And for how long?

Should I jump
Or let go?

That is the question before me.

Should I go back,
Return
From whence I came,
And erect an edifice
Bearing my likeness
And my name?

William S. Peters, Sr.

What is this vanity
That reflects upon me
As I look
Into this emptiness,
This void
That has no identity
Save the promise
Of rainbows and light?

Is this where truth sleeps,
While waiting for
Us, feeble ones
To awaken?

The forsaken ones
Are none other but ourselves, I think.
For are we not our own progenitors,
The ones who proffer
What and how
We prefer to live?

Where do the actualizing thoughts
Come from?

Are they innate
As are our proverbial souls?
Or is it more or less
A faction of our dream-state
That slips from the etheric dimensions
Into this thick 3-D soup
Where everything moves slow
And slowly
And slower?

I too once believed
There was more
Hidden in the
Scriptures, Suras, Verse and Prophesy
That a time of redemption
Would come soon.
Am I but an imagination
Of my own making,
Or is there truly more
Than meets my weakened eyes?
Or will all that has haunted me
Surprise me
And manifest,
As I have been told . . . taught?

I consider this and these things . . .

Where is Mom and Dad,
And Grammy and Gramps?
Where have they gone
When they crossed that
Dimensional bridge
From life unto . . .

Is the soup there lighter,
Easier to navigate?
Or is it but another place
Where one gets stuck,
Attempting to embrace its expression,
And come to a conscious understanding
Of what our paths are
And why?

Is there purpose
Behind the curtain
That has yet to be raised?

My, how I find the delicate tapestry
So intriguing!

I consider this and these things . . .

Who wishes to dance with me?

Did she have a white dress on?

Of Reason

I sit here now,
Laughing the tears away,
Casting the fears away,
Patiently waiting
For that new day
When all is as it should be.

We have endured much
Over the years,
Allowing the anguish
Of living
To wear upon us.

We have trusted,
Unfortunately,
In the wrong things
And the songs that
The demons and sirens
Sing.

Broken-winged angels
Sit amongst us,
And have foretold
Of this coming time
Of lamentations.
For the situation
At hand
Is almost beyond our control.

Protect your soul,
My friend!
For in the end,
That is all that you must
Account for.

William S. Peters, Sr.

The door to Armageddon
Has been taken off of the hinges,
And the walls
Of our self-induced ignorance
Have been obliterated
That we may see . . .
Yet many refuse to,
And have recused themselves
From the courts of justice.
So, 'just us' fools, jesters and imps
Are left behind
To mind the storehouse
And the last
Vestiges
Of reason.

It Is

Now and then
When and how
I come to the altar
And take a bow

    Before thyself
    A time-reverence
    Clarity of mind
    Succinct the sense

        A breath yet taken
        What I have to give
        That those to come
        May prosper, may live

            We dance in being
            Of thy own light
            To and fro, child,
            With wings of flight

                The tune doth play
                It always will
                Silence, golden
                Peace be still

                    Life and death
                    The twins of all
                    Listen, my child,
                    Take heed the call

William S. Peters, Sr.

Reflect within, tell
What thy see
From the halls of darkness
None can flee

The ocean waits
For all to return
Let loose thy judgement,
You need not discern

Trust is implicit
I thought you knew
The writings on the wall
Bid thee thy cue

It is what it is
And has always been
Never mind the demons
For thy heaven's within

It is!

Meeting Me

I had this longing,
Desire,
Aching, want . . .
I wanted to meet 'ME'.

I was lost truly!

Where does one go
To encounter one's self?
How does one
Come to know the
Truth of all truths, such as
"Who am I"
And "why"?

How about "where am I"?

Am I my laughter?
Am I my tears?
Am I my doubts?
Am I my fears?

Am I my inanity,
My insanity, my sanity?
Or am I my vanity?

What was it that constitutes
Who I am?
Was it me?
If so,
Where did I get
The instructions
To erect my self
In such a way?

William S. Peters, Sr.

By the way,
Where is the roadmap
Of the 'way'?

The song says,
'Oh, say, can you see'.
I cannot.
So, why is that my anthem?
Is it geographical only?

Am I lonely?
How would I know,
Except when I indulge
In a sort of
Self-expressive
Self-pity?

I dance to escape.
I sing to exhort.
I laugh to repress
Those things
That address my mirth,
My melancholy
And all of that which lies
In-between
The seen
And the unseen.
You know what I mean.

Shape up!

It is time for all . . .
Yes, ALL
Alter Egos
Within me
To step up their game
And become
TEAM PLAYERS.

As of RIGHT NOW,
We are,
I AM,
Evicting all dissenting voices
Who speak words
That lend themselves
To my stumbling,
Failure,
Or demise . . .
It is time for us
Collectively
To RISE UP
To become the 1
We were meant to be!

Our cause and purpose
IS . . .
2 B unified
In the field
Of love and affluence.

It makes no sense
For me to attempt
To continue

To feed and nurture you,
If you are not
Doing so for me.

After all,
I have enough things
Already vying
For the dying
Of my dreams,
While tongues go about
Lying
All over the place
About any and every
Little and BIG thing.

I want to sing songs
Of celebration,
Not lament
About what could have been.

So,
Note that NOTICE
Has been served.
I will be working towards
What I deserve,
And for you too.

The world deserves the
Best of me,
And you too.
I will no longer tolerate
The pirates aboard
My ship.

So, shape up,
Or ship the 'F' out!

A 20-20 voice in the wilderness

"I lay down my life that I may pick it up again for 'I' have the power to do so" ~ JC

A Poem for This Day and Those to Come

It was not until
I was assigned
To write a poem
About Jean Henry Dunant & Frédéric Passy
That I became keenly aware
Of who they were.

So, I beg your indulgence!
For my offering
May not be much of a poem,
But most certainly
Their lives were,
And still are!

You see,
Somewhere within their psyche,
Their dreams, beliefs
And their hopes
For a better way,
They were inspired
To create,
Just as they have done for me here,
As I attempt to
Share with you
A bit about
Who they are,
And how they continue
To affect you & me.

Jean Henry Dunant
Saw a red cross
As a symbol,
And thus, brought it to life
For the purposes

Of aiding those
Who were in need.
Yes, he, like perhaps you and me,
Was driven
To see his vision work,
Whereas
Frédéric Passy
Was not passé
In the least.
For he believed
That peace was
Something
We all deserved.

He joined leagues
With others such as himself,
And "The League of Peace"
Was born.

So, in conclusion,
And to avoid any confusion
As to what my poem may offer,
Read through this volume
And visit the offered links
In the front of the book
To learn more.
I implore you
To do so.

As I am,
Stay tuned, for each month.
We all shall learn something
About some of the
Recipients of
The Nobel Peace Prizes.

Legacy

When it comes to our mortality,
All 'class' flies
Out the window.

Your money or station
Cannot save you,
Nor can the neighborhood
You live in,
Or the car you drive.

Your 401K, stocks, investments
Will not buy safe passage.
Will they?

The playing fields
Have been leveled . . .
By you,
Without your complicity,
But by your greed
And stupidity.

Death is coming for you!

It may not be a virus,
But surely
None can escape
Her scythe,
When she comes at harvest time.

Some will be the chaff
And some the grain,
And some the seed
For future feedings
Of the survivors.

What is your legacy, my friend?
Does it make a difference?

William S. Peters, Sr.

That Feeling

The seeds had been planted long ago
In the garden,
Where my heart and dreams collided,
Colluded and coalesced.

I did not want much . . .
But I wanted it all.

I wanted a companion
Who stood by me
Through trials, tribulations and troubles,
One who would also share
My joys, laughter and triumph,
The turbulence and the solitude,
The sunshine and the rain,
The darkness and the obscurities . . .
Someone to pollinate my blossoming self.

Spring should be coming soon,
I think.
I can feel it approaching
Ever so softly and slowly.

I cannot remain a simple
Multi-legged caterpillar.
For I stumble far too often.
No, I must change,
Change,
Grow wings
That I may fly above
This dismality
My forlorn heart
Has struggled not to accept
As my norm.

No, I WILL not!

That feeling that lingers here
In the deepest recesses
Of my being
Is crying to be loosened,
Clawing at the doors of its prison,
Calling for the jailer, me,
To unlock the gate.

That feeling
Is not easily
Done away with.
No, that feeling
Grows in me,
Threatening my peace like shame
That I have acquired
In my acceptance of the 'Status Quos'
As my way,
As my way,
As my way
That will help me one day,
I pray,
To accomplish
That Feeling.

Until Now

I never really looked at the grass
The way I do now.

I never considered the gentle glow
Of the evening moon,
How it bathes me
And all that I see
In its embracing soft light.

I never really said, "thank you"
Before today
To all the bees
And other pollinators
Who do their duty
That we may partake abundantly
Of Mother's offerings.

I never looked so deeply
Into your eyes
And saw the sunshine
And profundity
Of your love
For me,
For us,
For family,
For friends,
For life . . .

Beautiful you are!

Until 'now,
I have never quite looked
At my life
With the reverence

For all that I have experienced
That has delivered me to 'here'
Until 'now'.

There is so much
I have not seen
Or noticed . . .
Until 'now'.

I am here . . . NOW!
I am watching.
I am taking notes.
I am sharing my 'Now' now!

Reclamation

We now have the opportunity
To reclaim our humanity,
Stolen by the rigors of life.

Yes, the strife
Will continue,
But the bigger picture,
The equation . . . we must figure
Out,
Has smacked us all
In the face
That the space
Between you and me
Can disappear,
Reappear
In the blink
Of an eye.

The farther apart we become,
The closer we become.

Dreams as delicate as gossamer
Are gently floating
On a wafting breeze.
Trees, mountains and the heavens
Are standing watch
Over the moving
Of man,
As they have done
Since the beginning.

They know of cycles,
As did the Buddha,
And our need

To step off
Of the 'Wheel of Suffering',
Where the only destinations are
Life and Death.

When will we awaken
And re-discover the core values
Of congruity,
Humanity,
And celebrate
Our reclamation?
When?

We, Poets

Some of us like to exact
Clever verse
With word-play
And obscure meanings,
Employing similes and metaphors,
Seeking cute and unusual adjectives
In our feeble attempts
To get the attention of our readers.

Words are our playground!

While others
Like to tell sweet nostalgic stories,
Some fictional, some not,
That emote memories
Of joy, pains and other
Emotional traipses
Back through
The annals of time.

Some of us like to write
Strictly about love or lust,
Or love and lust
Or lust,
And the love that manifests
From doing something
That makes us feel good.

And then there are those
Who write about
Our societal convictions,
Offering non-committal commentary
On relationship, history,
Politics, religion,

Or whatever other subject or theme
That strikes their fancy,
When they pick up
Their pen, phone, tablet, etc.

Oh, let us not forget
The 'Butterfly Writers'
Who speak of flowers,
Rainbows,
Hopes and dreams!

It seems to me
That any subject, theme
Is open and worthy
To poets
As they deem.

To be a poet
Means we must co-exist
With an inner conundrum
That beats a dichotomous drum
That is, at many times, attempting
To draw conclusions
And sums up the conditions of life
For ourselves
And that of others.

A seditious existence it is
Of us against me,
Me against myself
And all else
That wishes to contend
With the pretend
Of my peace.

William S. Peters, Sr.

Yes, we poets,
Are challenged
In many ways
To be the voice
Of the silent
And mostly unformulated thought
Of not only
Our fellow man,
But of thine own self.

Who was it that said,
"Know Thyself"?
He must have been
A poet at heart too!

Oh, we poets . . .

The End

Suspiring slowly,
Cautious with the conquer
Of each breath taken,
Acrimoniously acrid,
Ardently acuteness aside . . .

There was an air
Of ominous intent,
Paying obeisance
To his fears,
Which edified
His ego,
Which lauded its
False sense of power
Over his balanced belligerence.

The hands of time
Stayed their ways,
While whispering of past lore
They had stored
In the shadows
Where demons
Dare not go.

The Lordes and servants
Were obliviously engaged
In their dismissive duties
Of the day . . .
And the 'last breath'
Loomed at the edge,
Awaiting its turn
To declare
Its presence.
Flashes of brilliance

Flittered and fluttered
Into recognition
Here and there,
Offering a light
That cannot be held.
For even its truth
Was but as a whisping wind
That rustles the leaves of trees
Every now and then.

Sound was silenced
By its own doing.
For it had tired
Of listening
To the roteful
Incantations of life
It was sentenced to enunciate
Since the vault of the void
Had been opened.

First word is the last,
And the last
Shall be the first,
As a new age now
Is heralded in
But yet once again.

All that is left to do
Is to breathe
Until you cannot
Anymore.

The End

Epilogue

I will not remain silent that you may remain comfortable !

www.iamjustbill.com

about William S. Peters, Sr.

A 2016 and 2019 nominee for the Pulitzer Poetry Prize, William S. Peters, Sr., AKA 'just bill', has devoted himself to poetry with the onset of 1966. Since the day he became a dedicated voice in making his creative expression public – regardless of form, he has held the passionate conviction that the written art is a necessity. The author's spiritual essence reflects in his social actions, all of which serve his efforts to ease his personal angst and to contribute toward the betterment of humanity and the reconciliation of its plight.

To date, Peters authored more than 55 books. His poems have been published in excess of 220 anthologies, newspapers and literary magazines. In September 2015, the author was recognized as the "Poet Laureate" at the Kosovo International Poetry Festival. His sizeable book, *The Vine Keeper* was awarded The Golden Grape Award and showcased in Rahovec, the festival's center. Being so inspired by this communion of poets, Peters penned a book of tribute, *O Sweet Kosovo . . . Dreams of Rahovec*. This work has been since translated into Albanian by Fahredin Shehu – an esteemed poet and scholar, and was incorporated into the Rahovec School System in 2017.

From the 2015 inaugural formal introduction into the world of international poetry onward, invitations to William S. Peters, Sr. grew in speed and frequency. In 2016, he attended the Morocco International Poetry Festival in Rabat as an invited participant and a Keynote speaker. In 2017, the author's journey continued through a dazzling tour of Strumica, Macedonia; Monastir, Tunisia; Casablanca and Larache, Morocco; Istanbul, Turkey; Rome, Italy; Amman, Jordan; Bethlehem, Mar Saba, Ramallah and West Bank, Palestine, and Chicago, USA.

The author has been inspired in his travels to such great extent that he composed a large number of poems and prose pieces during and after his introduction to the places of his personal experiencing. Several resulting poetry collections have been included in *Morocco Love*; *Tunisia, My Love*, and *7 Days in Palestine . . . the Land, the People, the Blood, the Tears and the Laughter*. Peters was commissioned to write the book on Tunisia. It was launched in 2018 at the Poetry by the Sea Festival in Monastir, Tunisia.

William S. Peters, Sr. is the founder of Inner Child Press International, and currently serves as the CEO of Inner Child Enterprises, Ltd.; Managing Director of Inner Child Press International; Executive Producer of Inner Child Radio, and Executive Editor of Inner Child Magazine. He has published a multitude of first-time writers from across the globe through hands-on assistance, counseling and guidance, thus introducing a large body of literary work to the public. In its brief history, Inner Child Press International – Peters' publishing enterprise has brought global attention to a vast number of poets by means of official releases and inclusion of their craft in numerous anthologies.

The author's undertakings under his publisher-cloak encompass notable anthology series of global endeavors, including the voluminous *World Healing, World Peace* – published every two years since 2012, and *The Year of the Poet* – a monthly book, as conceived in January 2014 and published every month since. In the latter anthology, which is continuously thriving in its 7th year under Bill's unimpeachable leadership, The Poetry Posse, a core group of contributors, comprises between 14 and 18 writers from different world regions. In addition to accomplishing such a diverse representation of writers across the globe, this publication also features four guest poets each month.

William S. Peters, Sr. has received recognition for his work at large – publishing as well as writing also in the U.S., his country of birth. His appearances on North American radio and television shows are too copious to list here. His poetic work has been published in various countries of the world, including Kosovo, Albania, Germany, Iran, Iraq,

India, The Philippines, Taiwan, Canada, Italy, Romania, Saudi Arabia, Jordan, Morocco, Italy, England, Romania, France, and Poland. The author is known to be adamant about taking time out to share his humanitarian, spiritual and philosophical insights wherever he is invited. He has cited and performed his poetry at a variety of venues, such as summer camps for children, teacher workshops, poetry workshops and classrooms, including an October 2017-lecture to graduate students at The University of Jordan in Amman, Jordan.

In addition to composing poetry, the author has one other life-time passion: to induct underrepresented cultures into the mainstream entity of the "West". To materialize this predilection, he has – among other globally collaborative works, published *Voices from Iraq*, *Kurdish Voices*, *Aleppo*, *Palestine*, and the encyclopedic *Balkan Anthology*. In his own words: he has been 'building bridges of cultural understanding' throughout his career as a poet and publisher.

In 2019, William S. Peters, Sr. has authored *Eclectic Verse*, another voluminous book of poems. His creative writings in 2020 include the five volumes of *The Book of krisar*. He is presently working on two new poetry books, with multiple additional manuscripts waiting for their turn. All along, his presence is also sought out in a growing number of new anthologies.

Peters says: "I have always likened Life to that of a Garden. So, for me, Life is simply about the Seeds We Sow and Nourish. All things we 'Think and Do', will 'Be' Cause and eventually manifest themselves in an 'Effect' within our own personal 'Existences' and 'Experiences' . . . whether it be Fruit, Flowers, Weeds or Barren Landscapes!" In high regard of the "Fruits of his Labor", William S. Peters, Sr. wishes that everyone would thus go on to plant "Lovely Seeds" on "Good Ground" in their own "Gardens of Life".

unir1

a few words from Bill

hülya n. yılmaz [sic] is a noted and celebrated literary professional by her own rights. She has had a stellar academic career, teaching languages, cultures and literatures, penning and authoring scholarly treatises and books as well as designing courses in and for academia for a period over 40 years. It is a high honor to have one of her caliber participate in the production of my humble offerings. Please, take the time to read her awesome personal biography (following) and get to know her on a more intimate basis. She herself has contributed to an extensive collection of literary journals and anthologies and authored books, including her latest *Letter-Poems from a Beloved* (prose poetry in English) as well as other titles, such as *Canlarım, My Lifeblood* (poetry in English and Turkish with her own English translations), *this and that* (poetry in English), *Aflame* (memoirs in English verse), *Trance* (a tri-lingual book of poetry with her own English translations), and *An Aegean Breeze of Peace* (poetry in English, co-authored).

About the Editor

Penn State Liberal Arts Emerita, hülya n. yılmaz [sic] has enjoyed an extensive academic career. Advanced-level creative writing represents her primary area of teaching expertise. Her academic publications and treatises dwell on the literary reflections of cross- and inter-cultural influences – between the West and the Islamic East, in particular.

yılmaz has served as editorial consultant for a large number of academic and non-academic manuscripts of national and international significance with her substantial experience in book evaluations, critiques, developmental editing and translations. She is a longtime member of the Editorial Freelancers Association and the Academy of American Poets, Co-Chair and the Director of the Department of Editing Services at Inner Child Press International, Literary Translator (English, German and Turkish), Ghostwriter, and Book Reviewer.

A native of Turkey, hülya came to the U.S. in pursuit of a doctoral degree. After completing her dissertation at The University of Michigan, she has published *Das Ghasel des islamischen Orients in der deutschen Dichtung* (*The Ghazal of the Muslim Orient in German Literature*). This book emerged from her comprehensive research on the influences of Rumi and Hafiz on the 19th and 20th century mainstream German literature. Among her numerous scholarly discourses and national and international conference presentations, her chapter in a book, published by Palgrave McMillan of the US, stands out: "Orhan Pamuk: The Imagined Exile". In this publication, hülya examines the 2006 Nobel Prize for Literature recipient Orhan Pamuk's highly acclaimed novel, *Snow* within the context of Sufism, i.e. Islamic mysticism and the emigrational conceptualizations in Germany and Turkey as reflected in literature.

yılmaz's writing debut for public was launched with the publication of several of her poems in *Pastiche*, a regional literary journal that welcomes creative writings in different genres. She has authored *Trance* – a trilingual book of poetry with her own translations in English; *Aflame, Memoirs in Verse* and *this and that* – both, collections of poems in English; *Canlarım. My Lifeblood* (private edition) – a poetry book in Turkish and English with her own translations; *Letter-Poems from a Beloved* – prose poetry in English, and *An Aegean Breeze of Peace* – poems in English, which she has co-authored. *The Year of the Poet*, now in its seventh year, is an international anthology to which hülya contributes every month with three poems.

hülya has presented some of her poetic work in- and outside the U.S., including Kosovo, Canada, Jordan and Tunisia. Her poetry has been published in an excess of one hundred thirty-four anthologies of global endeavors. Two of her poems were distinguished on April 15, 2017 through inclusion in a U.S.-wide poetry exhibition, *Telepoem Booth*. On May 25, 2018, WIN (The Writers International Network of British Colombia, Canada) honored hülya with a 'poetry excellence' award. On March 1st, 2019, yılmaz performed poetry as an invited guest at the Turkish Consulate in observation of UNESCO's World Poetry Day, commemorating Attila Ilhan – a prominent Turkish poet.

yılmaz is currently working on various book-length literary manuscripts, including *homeland . . . a woman of the third space* – poetry in Turkish and English with her own translations, *Once upon a Time in Turkey . . .* – a collection of short stories within the context of autobiographical fiction, and *For the Sake of a Necklace* – a novel that is being constructed as fictional autobiography. Her short prose, including feature articles, book reviews, professional prefaces, introductions, forewords and epilogues, has appeared in publications of national and international makeup.

hülya says, she finds it vital for everyone to understand a deeper sense of self and that she writes creatively to attain and nourish a more comprehensive understanding and development of our humanity.

hülya's Web Links

Web Site (Creative Writing)
hulyanyilmaz.com

Web Site (Editing)
hulyasfreelancing.com

Facebook (Creative Writing)
www.facebook.com

Facebook (Editing)
www.facebook.com/hulyasfreelancing

Inner Child Press Author's Page
www.innerchildpress.com/h%C3%BClya-n-yilmaz

Inner Child Press Chief Editor's Page
www.innerchildpress.com/editing-services

Editor's Email
innerchildpresseditingservices@gmail.com

Author's Email
choiceandcourage@gmail.com

A Selection
of Other Books
by the Author

Available at:

www.innerchildpress.com

www.iamjustbill.com

and other fine bookstores

*For more of William S. Peters, Sr., visit his
personal web site at:* www.iamjustbill.com

7 Days

in

Palestine

william s. peters sr.

Eclectic Verse

mommy i hear those whispers . . . again

WilliAM s. Peters, sR.

William S. Peters, Sr. . . . . presents

the Wind . . .
        the Mountain . . .
                and the Sage . . .

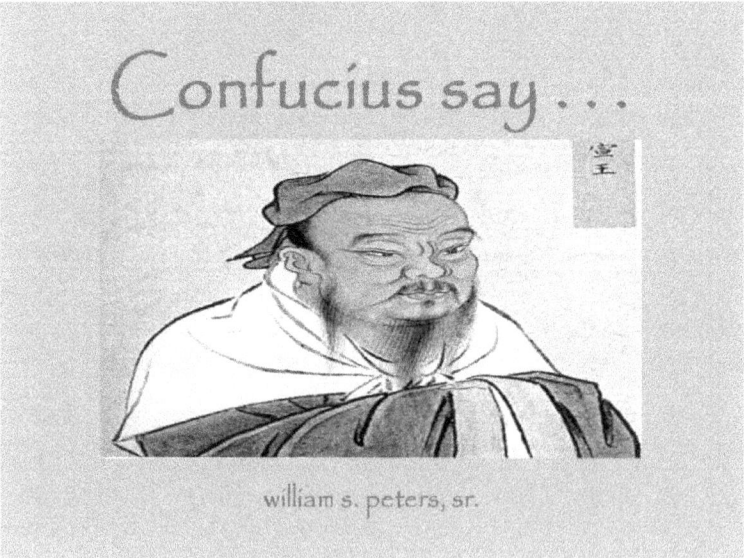

Confucius say . . .

william s. peters, sr.

Morocco L♥ve

william s. peters, sr.

المغرب ــ حُبّي

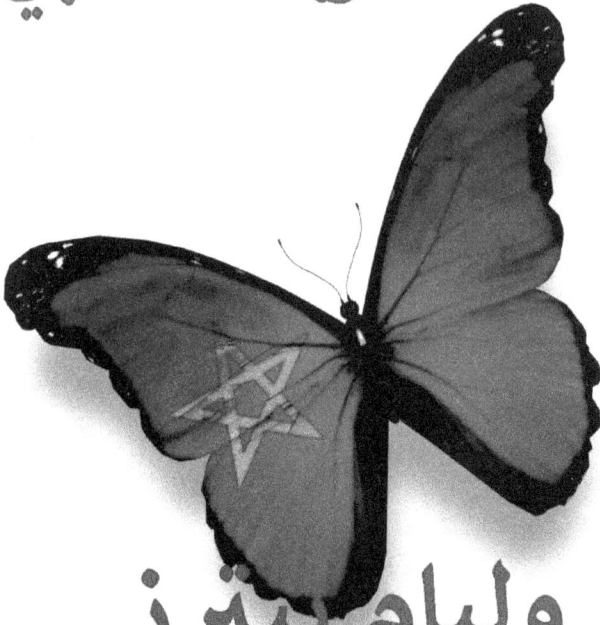

وليام بيترز

ترجمة: نزار سرطاوي

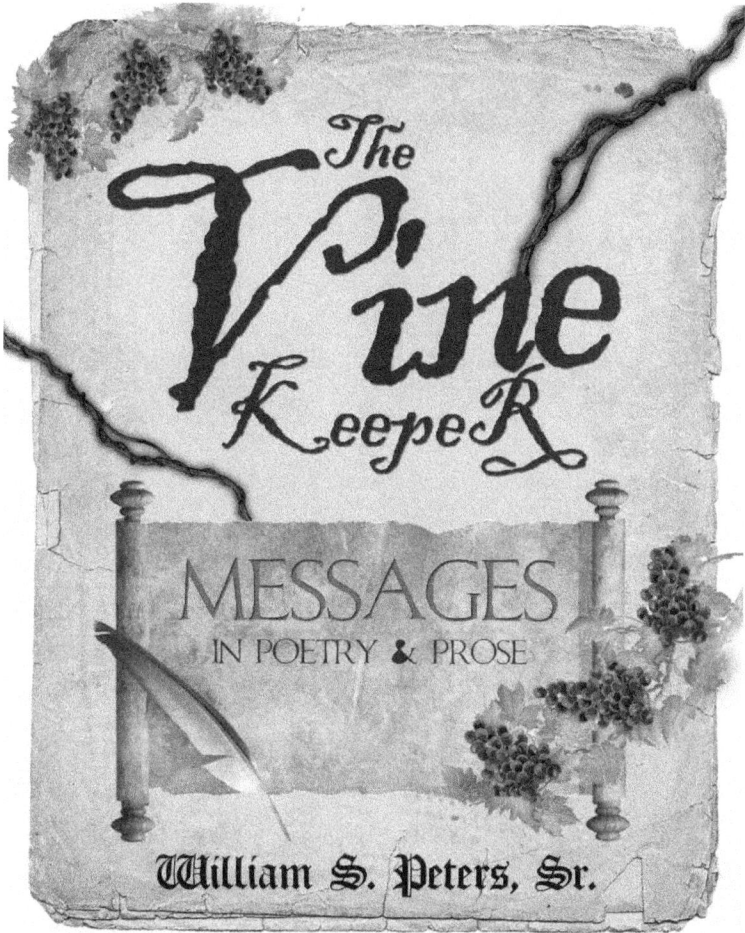

The Vine Keeper

MESSAGES
IN POETRY & PROSE

William S. Peters, Sr.

INNER CHILD PRESS

THIS IS WHY I
SLEEP

william s. peters sr.

INNER CHILD PRESS

Stories and Fables
and quaint little tales

William S. Peters, Sr.

Notes

from the

Coffee Table

. . . reflective moments from when things change.

William S. Peters, Sr.

O Sweet Kosovo

...dreams of Rahovec

Poetry & Prose

by

William S. Peters, Sr.

Think

on

These Things

Witticisms . . .
Thoughts
and other
Ramblings

stuff to think about
by

William S. Peters, Sr.

This Too Shall Pass

a spiritual poetic journey

with

William S. Peters, Sr.

inner child press
presents

Tunisia My Love

william s. peters, sr.

Day
by
Day

flowers and thorns

the Conscious
and
Spiritual Journey

of

William S. Peters, Sr.

Myiya Imani Rai

Inward Reflections

Think on These Things
Book II

william s. peters, sr.

The Book of krisar

Volume I

william s. peters, sr.

The Book of krisar

Volume II

william s. peters, sr.

The Book of krisar
Volume III

william s. peters, sr.

The Book of krisar
Volume IV

william s. peters, sr.

The Book of krisar

volume v

william s. peters, sr.

Inner Child Press

Inner Child Press is a publishing company founded and operated by writers. Our personal publishing experiences provide us an intimate understanding of the sometimes-daunting challenges writers, new and seasoned may face in the business of publishing and marketing their creative "Written Work".

For more information:

Inner Child Press

www.innerchildpress.com

intouch@innerchildpress.com

Inner Child Press International

'building bridges of cultural understanding'

202 Wiltree Court, State College, Pennsylvania 16801